The Waterfront Cookbook

Secrets of San Francisco Restaurant Chefs

Joseph Orlando

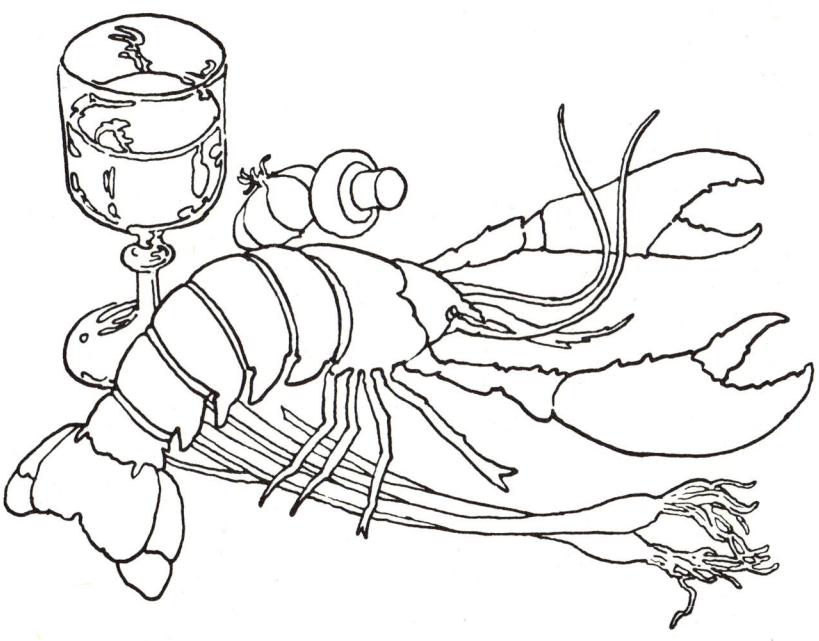

Property Of
Chicago Center
1515 E. 52nd Pl. Chicago, IL
773-363-1312
www.chicagocenter.org

A California Living Book

Illustrations: Tom Cervenak

Revised Edition

Copyright ®1980 California Living Books, The San Francisco Examiner Division of The Hearst Corporation, Suite 223, The Hearst Building, Third and Market Streets, San Francisco, California 94103.

Design/Production by David Charlsen.

All rights reserved. No part of this book may be reproduced in any form or by any electronic or mechanical means, including information storage and retrieval systems, without permission in writing from the publisher, except by a reviewer who may quote brief passages in a review.

Printed in the United States of America.

Library of Congress Catalog Card Number   80–66582

ISBN 0-89395-045-9 (paper)
ISBN 0-89395-063-7 (spiral binding)

Contents

Foreword 6

RESTAURANTS AND RECIPES 7
  Alfredo's 7
    Shrimp Bisque
  Alioto's No. 8 8
    Sautéed Lobster Tails
    Crab Mornay en Casserole
  N. Alioto's Captain's Cabin Restaurant 10
    Crab Legs Sauté
    Frankie's Special Salad
  Peter Alioto's Restaurant 11
    Calamari con Pomodoro (Squid with Tomatoes)
    Oysters alla Salvadori
  Amadeo's Oyster House 13
    Fillet of Petrale Milanese
  Borruso's Lighthouse Seafood Grotto 14
    Sauce ala Creole
    Lobster Thermidor
  Castagnola's Restaurant 16
    Calamari Calabresse
    Broiled Scallops
    Calamari Sicilian Style
    Calamari Sautéed
    Bar Balued Prawns
    Crab Creole
  Di Maggio's Restaurant 19
    Vongole Bianco (Clams with Spaghetti)
    Baked Sea Bass Visi Blanc
    Sautéed Lobster Tails

Exposition Fish Grotto   21
   Halibut (or Bass) with Egg Sauce
   Baked Sea Bass with Shrimp
   Chef Art Davis's Crab Olympics Award-
      Winning Crab Cioppino
   Crab Mornay
Fisherman's Grotto   27
   Cioppino Sauce
   Chef's Special Salad Dressing
Franciscan Restaurant   29
   Jumbo Prawns Sauté Marsala
   Crab Legs Sauté
Gaylord India Restaurant   31
   Gaylord Chicken Curry
   Gaylord Fried Okra with Cumin
Ginza Suehiro   34
   Chawan-Mushi (Egg Custard)
   Shabu-Shabu
Hayes Street Grill   37
   Calamari (Squid) Salad
   Ceviche
Humphrey's Seafood Bar and Grill   39
   Italian Cream
   Rice Pilaff
The Mandarin   41
   Fillet of Rock Cod, with Sweet and Sour
      Sauce
   Scallops Fu Yung
   Sweet and Sour Fish
Modesto Lanzone's   46
   Agnolotti
   Scampi
Restaurant Nakamura   49
   Gyoza (Japanese Egg Roll)
   Teppan Yaki Sauces

Nantucket Half Shell Restaurant 52
   Nantucket Bay Scallops Sautéed
Neptune's Palace 53
   Neptune's Palace Delight
   Neptune's Palace Scallops Sauté with Snow Peas
Old Swiss House 55
   Pgules au Whiskey
Pepe's on the Pier 56
   Chile con Queso
   Hot Sauce Dip
Rolf's Since 1960 58
   Zwiebelfleisch (Grilled Tenderloin with Onions)
   Rahm Schnitzel (Veal Cutlets with Cream and Mushrooms)
   Paprika Schnitzel (Veal Cutlets with Paprika)
The Rusty Scupper Restaurant 62
   Broiled Salmon Fillets with Hollandaise
   Scallops Morando
   Chinese Shrimp Scampi
A. Sabella's Restaurant 64
   Stuffed Turbot with Deviled Crab
   Crabmeat with Spaghetti
   Stuffed Swordfish Antone
Sabella and La Torre 68
   Crab Newburg Supreme
   Shrimp Rarebit
   Prawns Patriced
   Salmon a l'Orlando
Sam's Grill and Seafood Restaurant 72
   Clams Elizabeth
   Deviled Crab ala Sam
   Hangtown Fry

Scoma's   75
   Canneloni (with Seafood Filling)
   Sole Fish ala Via Reggio
   Abalone Bordelaise
Scott's Seafood Grill and Bar   79
   Fisherman's Stew
   Broiled Salmon
Sea Of Cortez   81
   Bouillabaisse
   Clam Chowder
Shang Yuen Restaurant   83
   Prawns a la Szechwan
Shipboard Restaurant   85
   Shrimp Paulette
Stradel's Fish Grotto   86
   Sweet and Sour Salmon Steaks
   Fried Sand Dabs
   Fried Abalone Steak
Swiss Louis Restaurant   88
   Frittata a la Louis
   Rex Sole Meunière with Capers
   Pesto Sauce
   Tripe
   Wild Duck
Tarantino's Restaurant   93
   Tarantino's Lazy Man's Cioppino
   Crab and Turbot
Tokyo Sukiyaki   95
   Sukiyaki
   Teriyaki
   Tempura
Vannelli's Seafood   99
   Vannelli's Fisherman's Stew
The Waterfront Restaurant   100
   Thrasher Shark, Sautéed and Capered
   California Rock Cod
   Crayfish

White Whale Restaurant 102
    White Whale Papillote
Yet Wah Mandarin Cuisine 104
    Lemon Chicken Yet Wah Style
    Yet Wah Special Lamb

DALMATIAN FISH COOKERY 108
Sand Dabs and Rex Sole, Fried on a Grill 111
Dominic Ivelich's Fried Sand Dabs 111
Charcoal Broiled Fish 111
Boiled Sea Bass Dalmatian 112
Ernie Aviani's Cioppino 114

BASIC RECIPES 115
Hollandaise Sauce 115
Cream Sauce 115
Brown Sauce 116
Fish Stock 116
Tartar Sauce 117
Cocktail Sauce 117

HOW TO BUY A FISH 118
Selecting Fresh Seafood 119
Frozen Seafood 121
Storing Fish 122
How to Prepare Live Crabs and Lobsters 123
Abalone 123

BEST BAY AREA SEAFOOD MARKETS 124

INDEX OF RECIPES 136

Foreword

In prehistoric times, one of the ancestors of the human race discovered a piece of meat that had been exposed to flame. He or she tasted it and decided it was a marked improvement over the raw diet of the time. From such a random experience, the art of cooking was probably born. Since that happy day, people have continually searched for new and different ways to prepare food. The preparation of food has become a hobby for some, a livelihood for others, and a source of enjoyment for all. My hope is that the recipes in this book will tantalize your taste buds and bring you pleasure.

My forebears came from the craggy hills and sun-washed beaches of Sicily, an isolated island where food staples were limited but fish were abundant. This heritage set the stage for developing Italian cooking to a fine art in San Francisco where the abundance of seafood, spices, and other ingredients in this port city allowed full rein to the talents of Italian chefs. San Francisco is known the world over as a mecca for food lovers.

In this guide to good meals, we have collected recipes that have stood the test of time from the bleak landscape of Sicily to the blue waters of San Francisco Bay, always keeping in mind that gourmet cooking and eating may be enjoyed by all. These recipes will provide tantalizing taste experiences at a modest budget. *Bon Appétit!*

Joseph J. Orlando

Alfredo's

400 Jefferson
Fisherman's Wharf
San Francisco

Shrimp Bisque

1 pound shrimp
½ cup oil
½ cup butter
½ cup chopped leeks
½ cup chopped celery
½ cup finely chopped carrots
1 cup flour
2 quarts fish *fumet* (or Fish Stock)
2 cups white wine
1 cup sherry wine
5 chopped tomatoes
Salt, pepper, and cayenne to taste
2 cups cream
Fine herbs to taste
Butter to taste

Sauté the shrimp in the oil. Then add leeks, celery, carrots, and butter, and cook for 2 minutes. Add flour, raise heat, and stir constantly for a few minutes to make a paste. Then add heated Fish Stock (see page 116) add all wine, and stir the soup until it boils. Add tomatoes, salt, pepper, cayenne, and cream. Simmer slowly for one hour. Remove from fire. Add butter and herbs for enrichment. Purée and strain before serving.

Serves four to six.

Alioto's No. 8

Fisherman's Wharf
San Francisco

Sautéed Lobster Tails

Clean and peel six lobster tails. Sauté in garlic butter 6 to 8 minutes. Transfer to heated platter.

Heat a serving of cooked rice in the pan in which lobster was sautéed. Place in serving dish and arrange lobster tails on top. Cover with **Mustard Sauce** (see recipe below) and glaze under a broiler.

Serves three.

Mustard Sauce

1 cup Cream Sauce
1 tablespoon (prepared) mustard
1 teaspoon cold water

Mix mustard with water. Stir mixture into **Cream Sauce** (see page 115) about 2 minutes before serving. The quantity of mustard may be increased or decreased to make the flavor strong or mild as desired.

Makes 1 cup.

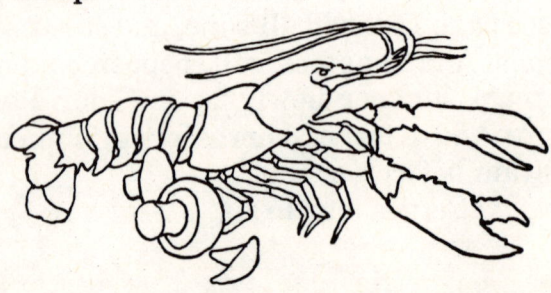

Crab Mornay en Casserole

2 cups rich Cream Sauce
2 teaspoons sherry wine
2 cups fresh cooked crabmeat
4 slices American cheese
Paprika, as desired
Melted butter, as required

Into each of four individual casseroles pour ½ cup **Cream Sauce** (see page 115), to which wine has been added. Add layer of ½ cup crabmeat, and top with a slice of cheese. Sprinkle each casserole with paprika and butter.

Bake in moderate oven (350 degrees) for 10 minutes, and serve hot.

Serves four.

N. Alioto's Captain's Cabin Restaurant

155 Jefferson
Fisherman's Wharf
San Francisco

Crab Legs Sauté

Dust one pound of crab legs in flour, and sauté quickly in 4 tablespoons of butter. Add sliced mushrooms and chopped green onions. Add a small amount of chopped canned tomatoes, salt, pepper, sauterne wine. Simmer for 5 minutes.
Serve on a bed of rice.
Serves four.

Frankie's Special Salad

This excellent recipe came from my mother, who made it on special days.
To one pound of crab or baby shrimp in a large bowl, add celery hearts, cut on a slant. Add one avocado, cut into slices. Season to taste with salt and pepper. Add olive oil and vinegar. Toss, and allow to stand in the refrigerator for at least 2 hours. Serve on lettuce, with a sliced tomato.
Serves four.

Peter Alioto's

Fisherman's Wharf
San Francisco

Calamari con Pomodoro (Squid with Tomatoes)

2 pounds squid
4 tablespoons olive oil
2 cloves garlic, chopped
Salt and pepper to taste
Pinch of oregano
½ cup dry sherry
1 cup solid-pack tomatoes
1 tablespoon chopped parsley

Thoroughly clean and wash squid, and cut into small pieces. Pour oil into saucepan and heat. Brown garlic about 3 minutes. Add squid. Cover, and sauté 10 minutes. Add salt, pepper, oregano, and sherry, and cook 10 minutes longer over low flame. Add tomatoes and parsley. Cook 15 minutes, or until tender.

Serves four to six.

Oysters alla Salvadori

2 dozen oysters
1 clove garlic
3 tablespoons butter
Salt and pepper to taste
1 cup bread crumbs
2 tablespoons olive oil
2 tablespoons chopped parsley
½ tablespoon oregano
Juice of one lemon

Scrub oyster shells; rinse in cold water. Insert knife between edges of shells, cutting through the muscle of oysters. Pry open, and remove oysters from shell.

Rub the half shells with garlic and tiny pieces of butter. Replace oysters in shells. Sprinkle with salt and pepper. Mix bread crumbs, oil, parsley, and oregano. Sprinkle mixture over each oyster. Arrange in pan, and bake in moderate oven for 10 minutes, or until edges of oysters curl. Serve hot with lemon juice.

Serves four to six.

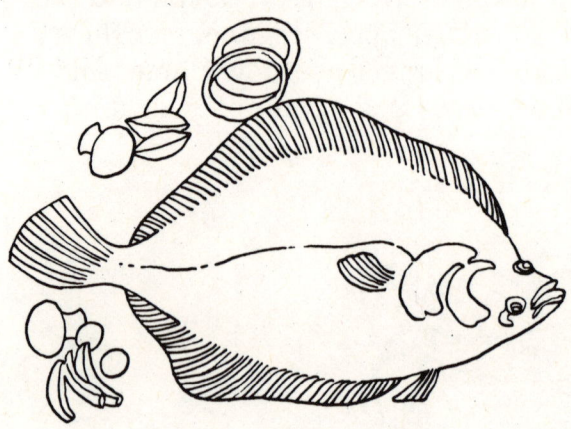

Amadeo's Oyster House

Pier 39
San Francisco

Fillet of Petrale Milanese

1½ cups bread crumbs
  1 large clove garlic, finely chopped
  1 tablespoon chopped parsley
  2 tablespoons grated Parmesan or Romano cheese
Salt and pepper to taste
  4 large petrale fillets
  2 well-beaten eggs
  6 tablespoons oil

Mix together bread crumbs, garlic, parsley, and cheese; season with salt and pepper. Dip the fish in egg. Roll it in bread crumb mixture, patting on the mixture, and fry on both sides in oil until nicely browned. Serve with cooked rice and boiled zucchini.
Serves four.

Borruso's Lighthouse Seafood Grotto

Fisherman's Wharf
San Francisco

Sauce ala Creole

2 cups onions, sliced julienne style
2 cups celery, sliced julienne style
3 tablespoons butter
2 cups tomato sauce
2 cups tomato purée or tomato paste
2 cups bell peppers, sliced julienne style
1 clove garlic, finely chopped
3 whole bay leaves
1 tablespoon oregano
1 tablespoon monosodium glutamate
1 teaspoon thyme
1 teaspoon salt
1 teaspoon pepper
2 cups beef stock or water

Braise onions and celery until half cooked in butter. Add tomato sauce, purée, peppers, garlic, bay leaves, oregano, monosodium glutamate, thyme, salt, and pepper. Simmer for 3 minutes, and add beef stock or water. Simmer for 2 hours, stirring frequently to keep sauce from sticking to bottom of pot.
Makes 1½ quarts.

Lobster Thermidor

1 pound lobster, diced
3 tablespoons butter
1 cup sliced mushrooms, canned or fresh
1 cup chopped onion or shallots
1 clove garlic, finely chopped
2 tablespoons chopped pimentos
1 tablespoon chopped parsley
½ teaspoon oregano
½ teaspoon monosodium glutamate
Salt and pepper to taste
½ cup sherry wine
Newburg Sauce
Grated Parmesan cheese

Sauté lobster in butter in a heavy saucepan. Add mushrooms, onions, garlic, pimentos, parsley, oregano, monosodium glutamate, salt and pepper, and wine. Cook for 2 minutes. Add **Newburg Sauce** (see recipe below).

Place mixture in lobster shells. Cover with grated Parmesan cheese or **Hollandaise Sauce** (see page 115), and bake for 15 to 20 minutes in 400-degree oven.

Serves two.

Newburg Sauce

Make a thick **Cream Sauce** (see page 115). Add coloring to acquire desired egg shade. Add wine to taste.

Castagnola's Restaurant

Jefferson and Jones
Fisherman's Wharf
San Francisco

Calamari Calabresse

2 pounds calamari
¼ cup olive oil
1 teaspoon finely chopped parsley
Salt and pepper to taste
Lemon juice (or vinegar) to taste

Clean calamari. Do not cut. Put the whole calamari in water, and boil for 10 minutes. Drain, dry, and put in deep bowl. Add oil, parsley, salt, pepper, and lemon juice or vinegar. Serve hot or cold.
Serves four to six.

Broiled Scallops

16 scallops
3 tablespoons oil
1 clove garlic, chopped
Salt and pepper to taste
Lemon, cut in quarters

Put scallops in a pie plate; add oil, garlic, and salt and pepper. Broil for 10 minutes. Then place on platter; add lemon and serve.
Serves two.

Calamari Sicilian Style

Clean calamari and cut into quarters; then fry in olive oil. Add salt and pepper and finely chopped garlic. Do not cook very long (about 10 minutes). When cooked, add parsley. Place on platter. Add lemon juice, to taste, and serve.

Calamari Sautéed

1 pound calamari
4 tablespoons olive oil
½ onion, chopped
6 fresh medium-sized mushrooms, sliced
Salt and pepper to taste
1 large clove garlic, chopped fine
¼ cup sauterne wine

Cut calamari in quarters; simmer in hot frying pan with oil for 2 or 3 minutes. Add onion, mushrooms, garlic, and salt and pepper to taste. Cook for 5 to 7 minutes. Raise flame to very high for 1 minute. Add wine, and let simmer for 2 minutes. Cooking time: 10 to 12 minutes altogether.
Serves two or three.

Bar Balued Prawns

12 large prawns
 4 tablespoons oil
 1 clove garlic, chopped
Salt and pepper to taste
 1 lemon, cut in quarters

Put prawns in a pie plate; add oil, garlic, and salt and pepper, and broil for 10 minutes. Place on platter; add lemon and serve.
Serves two.

Crab Creole

1 onion
1 clove garlic
3 pieces celery
2 tablespoons olive oil
Salt and pepper to taste
Flour, to thicken
2 no. 2 cans solid-pack tomatoes
1 no. 2 can tomato purée
Pinch of sweet basil, laurel, rosemary
Few grains of cayenne, paprika
Dash of Worcestershire sauce
1½ cups crabmeat

Dice onion, garlic, and celery. Sauté in olive oil until brown. Add seasonings and enough flour to thicken; then add tomatoes, purée, and herbs. Salt and pepper to taste, and cook 4 hours. When ready to serve, add crab. Cook for 10 minutes.
Makes 1 quart.

Di Maggio's Restaurant

Fisherman's Wharf
San Francisco

Vongole Bianco (Clams with Spaghetti)

48 coco clams, shelled
1 cup sliced mushrooms
½ cup chopped green onions
2 cloves garlic, finely chopped
1 cup Cream Sauce
Butter, to sauté
1¼ cups white wine
Salt and pepper to taste
Monosodium glutamate, to taste

Sauté mushrooms, onions, and garlic in butter until tender. Add wine and **Cream Sauce** (see page 115); stir until smooth.

Sauté clams in a separate pan in butter until tender. Mix all together, and pour over four orders spaghetti, cooked *al dente*.

Serves four.

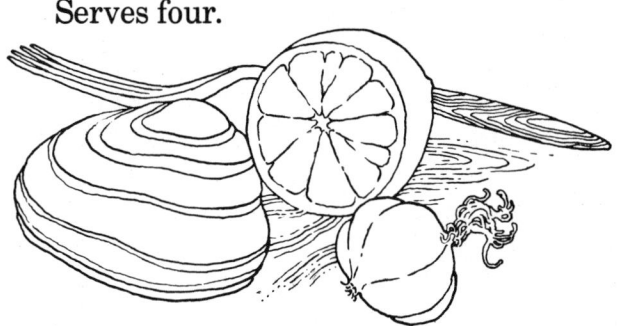

Baked Sea Bass Visi Blanc

4 12-ounce pieces fresh sea bass fillet
1 cup sliced mushrooms
½ cup chopped green onions
1 teaspoon thyme
Salt and white pepper to taste
½ cup sauterne wine
½ cup water

    Place sea bass in buttered casserole or pan. Sprinkle with mushrooms, onions, thyme, and salt and pepper. Pour wine and water over all, and bake in 350-degree oven until fish flakes. Serve at once.
    Serves four.

Sautéed Lobster Tails

4 Australian lobster tails
4 tablespoons butter
½ cup chopped green onions
1 cup sliced mushrooms
2 cloves garlic, chopped
½ teaspoon thyme
1 cup Cream Sauce
½ cup sherry wine
Salt and white pepper to taste

    Parboil lobster tails, and cut into bite-sized pieces. Sauté onions, mushrooms, garlic, thyme in butter. When tender, add wine and **Cream Sauce,** (see page 115), and mix until smooth. Fold in lobster pieces. Add salt and white pepper to taste. Serve with rice pilaff.
    Serves four.

Exposition Fish Grotto

Fisherman's Wharf
San Francisco

Halibut (or Bass) with Egg Sauce

2 pounds sliced halibut (or bass)
¼ teaspoon salt
Sprig of parsley
½ cup sauterne wine
½ cup chopped hardboiled egg
1 teaspoon chopped parsley

Place the fish, salt, parsley sprig, and wine in a shallow pan with just enough water to cover the fish. Poach the fish slowly for 10 minutes. Remove from the fire, and keep hot until ready to serve.

Prepare **Egg Sauce** (see recipe below).

Remove fish to platter. Pour sauce over fish. Sprinkle with chopped parsley and hardboiled egg, and serve.

Serves four.

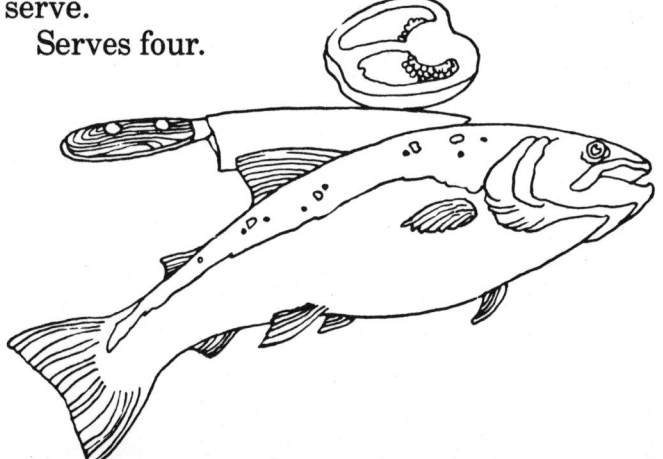

Egg Sauce

2 cups milk
½ cup chopped onion
1 teaspoon chopped shallots
¼ cup butter
¼ cup flour
Salt to taste
2 beaten egg yolks
1 cup California shrimp (optional)

Bring the milk to a boil. Set aside, keeping it hot. Sauté onions and shallots in butter in a saucepan until tender but not brown. Stir in the flour, and slowly add the hot milk. Stir briskly until the sauce is smooth. Simmer for 10 minutes. Add salt, and remove from fire. Stir in the beaten egg yolks. Add shrimp, if desired, and simmer 5 minutes more.

Baked Sea Bass with Shrimp

2 pounds sea bass, cut into six steaks
1 large potato, sliced very thin
Juice of two lemons
½ cup dry white wine
2 teaspoons salt
¼ teaspoon pepper
2 crushed bay leaves
3 tablespoons olive oil
2 onions, finely cut
1 teaspoon chopped shallots
½ cup button mushrooms
1 no. 2½ can tomatoes with purée
½ cup finely chopped celery
½ pound California shrimp meat
½ cup grated Parmesan cheese
1 teaspoon parsley flakes
Butter

Wash and dry the fish. Arrange the steaks in a well-buttered pan or shallow casserole. Arrange the potato slices evenly over the fish. Sprinkle the lemon juice, white wine, salt, pepper, and bay leaves over the fish and potato. Let stand for 15 minutes or longer.

In a separate pan, sauté (in olive oil) onions, shallots, and mushrooms until the onions begin to brown. Add the tomatoes and celery. Let boil for 10 minutes. Pour sauce over fish and potatoes; sprinkle with shrimp. Top with cheese and parsley flakes and dot with butter. Bake at 350 degrees for 30 minutes.

Serves four.

Chef Art Davis's Crab Olympics Award-Winning Crab Cioppino

4 large live crabs and crab fat
3 cloves garlic, finely chopped
3 medium chopped onions
1 cup thinly sliced celery
1 cup button mushrooms
¼ cup olive oil
½ cup chopped parsley (washed and squeezed after chopping)
3 crushed cloves
2 teaspoons salt
½ teaspoon black pepper
2 large crushed bay leaves
¼ teaspoon oregano
¼ teaspoon sweet basil
1 teaspoon paprika
Sprig fresh rosemary
¼ teaspoon dill seed
3½ cups stewed tomatoes
½ cup tomato paste
1 cup dry red wine
4 cups water (can vary)
1 pound large raw prawns
2 pounds raw clams, in the shell
1 large lobster tail, 12 to 14 ounces

Crack the crabs, saving all the fat from each crab. Sauté garlic, onions, celery, and mushrooms in the oil until vegetables are tender. Add all herbs and seasonings. Stir for a few minutes.

Add the tomatoes, tomato paste, wine, and water. Bring mixture to a rolling boil. Lower heat, and simmer the sauce for at least an hour. Add the crabs, crab fat, prawns, raw clams, and lobster tail, which should be sliced into ½-inch slices, and cook for another 12 to 14 minutes. The cioppino is ready as soon as the clams open.

Serves six to eight.

Suggestion: Buy only tightly closed clams, and peel the prawns only halfway toward the tail. The lobster tail may be sliced across so that the meat is completely thawed before adding to the cioppino. Your crab retailer will be glad to crack the crab and save the fat for you.

Crab Mornay

1 cup heavy cream
1 cup grated Parmesan cheese
1 cup soft jack cheese, grated or chopped fine
Crab butter
¼ cup dry sauterne wine
Salt and pepper to taste

Make **Bechamel Sauce,** (see recipe below), and keep hot. Make **Crab Fumet** (see recipe below).

To the Bechamel Sauce add 1 cup Parmesan cheese, jack cheese, crab butter saved from one raw crab, and the Crab Fumet. Stirring constantly, slowly add the cream. Never stop stirring until the cream thickens. Add wine and salt and pepper, stirring quickly. If it is necessary to thin the sauce a little bit, add a little more wine.

Place equal parts of crab meat and sauce in a casserole. Top with extra Parmesan cheese and a small amount of paprika; then dot with butter. Place casserole in preheated 350-degree oven. Bake for about 12 minutes, or until the cheese browns evenly.

Serves four to six.

Bechamel Sauce

1 cup chopped onions
Sprig of fresh thyme
½ teaspoon grated nutmeg
½ pound butter
½ cup flour
1½ quarts cold dairy cream

Sauté onions, thyme, and nutmeg in butter. When onions are tender and a light transparent color but not brown, add flour for the roux. Over very low heat, whipping constantly, slowly add a little more than a quart of cream. Whip until creamy thick. Strain, and keep hot.

Crab Fumet

2 live crabs
1 tablespoon water

Clean and crack crabs. Be sure to save the fat from one raw crab. (In San Francisco, this fat is called "crab butter.") Put both cracked crabs into a steamer, add a tablespoon of water, and cover. Steam for about 15 minutes. The crabs are cooked when the crab shells turn red. When done, pour the broth from the cooked crabs into a cup and save; pick the meat of the crab from the shell and save.

Fisherman's Grotto

No. 9 Fisherman's Wharf
San Francisco

Cioppino Sauce

½ cup olive oil
1½ cups chopped onions
  1 tablespoon chopped garlic
  1 tablespoon chopped parsley
  1 tablespoon celery
  1 tablespoon chopped green bell pepper
  2 cups solid-pack tomatoes
  1 cup tomato sauce
  2 tablespoons salt
  1 tablespoon black pepper
  1 tablespoon paprika
  ½ cup sherry wine
  3 cups water
Small sprig of fresh basilico

Braise onions, garlic, parsley, celery, and green bell pepper in oil until golden brown. Add tomatoes and tomato sauce, salt, black pepper, paprika, sherry wine, and basilico. Cook 15 minutes. Add water, and cook slowly for 1 hour.

This amount of sauce will serve six. Any fresh fish or shellfish may be used.

Chef's Special Salad Dressing

1½ cups chili sauce
¼ cup finely ground celery
¼ cup finely ground sour pickles
2 cups mayonnaise
1 teaspoon lemon juice
½ teaspoon Worcestershire sauce
1 teaspoon horseradish

Put all ingredients into bowl. Mix until well blended.

When stored in cool place, dressing will keep indefinitely. Do not refrigerate.

This dressing can be used on any seafood salad.

Makes 1 quart.

Franciscan Restaurant

Fisherman's Wharf
San Francisco

Jumbo Prawns Sauté Marsala

1 pound jumbo prawns
2 tablespoons cooking oil
1 chopped green onion
Pinch of whole rosemary
1 clove garlic, chopped
1 chopped white onion
¼ cup Marsala wine
½ cup Brown Sauce
Salt and pepper to taste

Peel and fantail prawns. Sauté in hot oil. Add green onion, rosemary, garlic, white onion, wine, **Brown Sauce** (see page 116), and salt and pepper. Lower heat, and simmer for 10 minutes. This seafood succulence is served with rice pilaff.
Serves two.

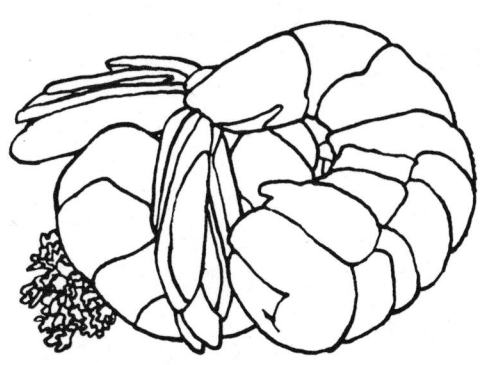

Crab Legs Sauté

  4 tablespoons butter
  ¼ pound sliced mushrooms
  1 clove garlic, chopped
  2 tablespoons chopped green onions
  1 chopped shallot
1½ pounds crab legs
Pinch of white pepper
  ¼ cup sherry wine
  ½ pint Brown Sauce

    Sauté, in butter, mushrooms, garlic, onions, and shallot until tender (about 5 minutes). Add crab legs, pepper, and wine. Continue to sauté. Reduce sherry until almost dry. Add **Brown Sauce** (see page 116), and simmer until hot and mixed.
    Serves six.

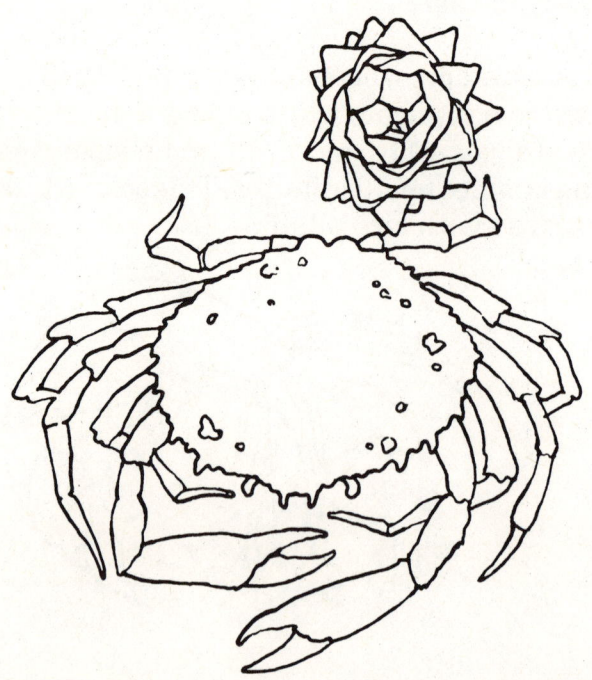

Gaylord India Restaurant

900 North Point
Ghirardelli Square
San Francisco

Gaylord Fried Okra with Cumin

2½ tablespoons *ghee* (clarified butter) or vegetable oil
1 medium onion, chopped
1 teaspoon salt
1 pound whole fresh okra
2½ teaspoons ground cumin
¼ teaspoon ground black pepper

In a heavy frying pan, heat *ghee* or oil until very hot. Add onions and salt, and stir for about 7 or 8 minutes until onions are light brown. Add okra, cumin, and pepper. Cook until okra is tender and most of the liquid has evaporated. Serve hot.
Serves four.

Gaylord Chicken Curry

6 tablespoons vegetable oil
3 pounds chicken, cut into pieces
¾ cup finely chopped onion
2½ teaspoons chopped garlic
1¾ teaspoons finely chopped fresh ginger
1 teaspoon ground cumin
½ teaspoon turmeric
1 teaspoon ground coriander
1 teaspoon cayenne
½ pound chopped tomatoes
1 tablespoon fresh, finely chopped green coriander
6 tablespoons unflavored yoghurt
2½ teaspoons salt
½ cup water
2½ teaspoons lemon juice
1 teaspoon *garam masala**

Garam masala is made by grinding finely together: 1 inch stick cinnamon, 6 green cardamons, 6 cloves, ½ teaspoon cumin seeds, ¾ teaspoon corianders, and ½ teaspoon black peppercorn.

In a large heavy frying pan, heat oil until it is very hot. Add chicken, and fry for 2 or 3 minutes. Transfer the chicken to a plate. Add onions, garlic, and ginger to the oil remaining in the frying pan, and fry for about 7 or 8 minutes, stirring constantly, until the onions are soft and golden brown. Reduce the heat to low. Add cumin, turmeric, ground coriander, cayenne, and 1 tablespoon water. Fry for 1 minute or so, stirring constantly; then add tomatoes, fresh coriander, yoghurt, and salt. Cook until the oil separates from the mixture. Add the chicken. Pour in the rest of the water. Bring to a boil, turning chicken in the sauce. Cook until chicken is tender. Pour lemon juice over the dish, and sprinkle with *garam masala*. Serve hot.

Serves four to six.

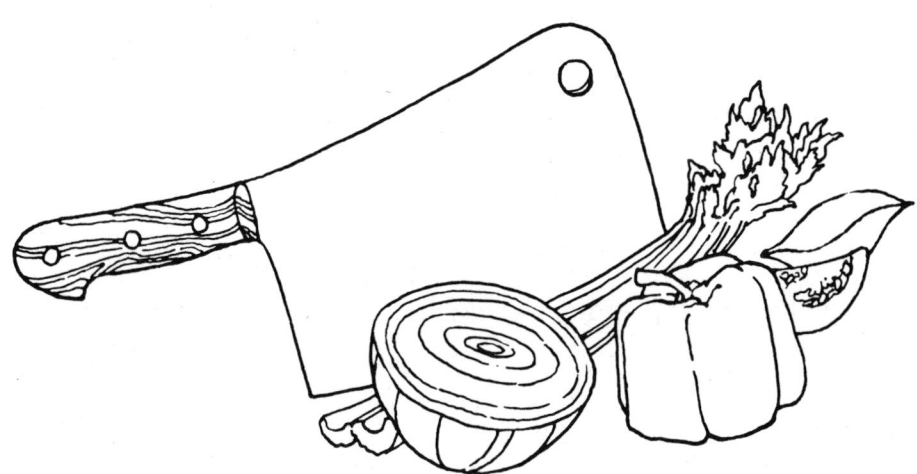

Ginza Suehiro

900 North Point
Ghirardelli Square
San Francisco

Chawan-Mushi (Egg Custard)

10 cups Basic Japanese Broth
¼ pound boneless chicken
5 prawns
10 pieces *ginnan* (ginkgo nut)
10 slices *kamaboku* (fishcake)
10 1-inch parboiled spinach stalks
8 eggs
1 tablespoon soy sauce
2 teaspoons salt
½ teaspoon monosodium glutamate

Make ten cups **Basic Japanese Broth** (see recipe below).

Cut chicken into 10 pieces. Devein prawns, slice lengthwise, and cut into quarters.

In each of ten custard cups, place two pieces prawn, a ginkgo nut, one piece chicken, a slice of fish cake, and one spinach stalk. Then, in a separate bowl, beat eggs. Add soy sauce, salt, and monosodium glutamate and stir beaten eggs into Basic Japanese Broth. Mix well. Pour custard cups 4/5 full. Place lids on cups, and steam 13 to 15 minutes, until custard is firm. Serve hot.

Serves ten.

Basic Japanese Broth

10 cups water
1 cup sliced bonito flakes
Dash of salt

Boil water; add the sliced bonito. Add a dash of salt. Boil ingredients until flakes settle. Take clear broth.

Shabu-Shabu

2½ pounds paper-thin sliced beef
½ head Chinese cabbage
2 ounces *harusame* (dried taro noodles)
1 bunch green onions
10 fresh mushrooms
2 pieces bamboo shoots
1 block *tofu* (soy bean curd)
1 carrot
1 large dried *konbu* (seaweed)

Slice the head of cabbage lengthwise into quarters, then cut into 1½-inch pieces. Soak *harusame* in hot water, rinse, and drain. Cut green onions into 1½-inch pieces. Cut carrot into 1½-inch slivers. Cut fresh mushrooms into quarters. Slice bamboo shoots lengthwise. Cut the *tofu* in half, then slice lengthwise.

Fill a pot (preferably a deep iron pot) ¾ full of hot water; add dried *konbu*. Boil. Place ½ portion of cut vegetables into kettle. When water boils, each guest may take a slice of beef and cook it to order. Dip cooked beef and vegetables in **Shabu-Shabu Dipping Sauce.**

Serves five.

Shabu-Shabu Dipping Sauce

3 cups broth
2 cups soy sauce
⅓ cup *secumir* (ground sesame seeds)
½ cup *mirin* (sweet *sake*)
½ teaspoon ground garlic
2 tablespoons half-and-half
⅛ teaspoon monosodium glutamate

Combine the above ingredients. Serve the dipping sauce in individual bowls.

Hayes Street Grill

324 Hayes Street
San Francisco

Calamari (Squid) Salad

3 pounds fresh calamari (1½ pounds cleaned)
2 thinly sliced red bell peppers
1 small red onion, thinly sliced
½ bunch parsley, finely chopped
6 cloves garlic, finely chopped
3 tablespoons capers
½ cup red wine vinegar
1 cup olive oil
Salt and pepper to taste
Juice of 1 or 2 lemons

Clean and cut calamari into rings, leaving tentacles whole. Drop into rapidly boiling salted water for 15 seconds, just until calamari turns white. If cooked longer, they will turn rubbery. Drain quickly and rinse in cold water. Drain again, and towel dry. Place in bowl; add bell pepper and onion.

Toss with parsley, garlic, capers, vinegar, and oil. Season with salt and pepper. Adjust seasoning with lemon juice.

To clean calamari: Pull out head and tentacles. Cut off tentacles above eyes. Squeeze tentacles to remove spherical bone. Put a finger in the mantle to pull out cellophanelike sword, or cuttle bone. Starting from the pointed tip of body, squeeze out the remaining inters. Wash in running water.

Serves six.

Ceviche

2 pounds fresh snapper or ling cod, boned and cut into small pieces
Lime and lemon juice
Small bunch of cilantro (Chinese parsley), chopped
3 chopped ripe tomatoes
1 chopped Bermuda onion
Hot sauce and salt to taste

Marinate fish in a marinade of equal parts of lime and lemon juice (enough to cover the fish). Marinate for 8 hours, or overnight. Add to the marinated fish the cilantro, tomatoes and onions. Season with hot sauce and salt, and serve.
    Serves four to five.

Humphrey's Seafood Bar and Grill

(No Longer Doing Business)

Pier 39
San Francisco

Italian Cream

1 quart milk
8 large eggs
1¼ cups sugar
1 whole orange rind
½ lemon rind
3 tablespoons vanilla extract
1 tablespoon almond extract

Scald milk. Break eggs into a bowl. Beat sugar into eggs; add milk slowly into eggs and sugar, stirring constantly. Strain through fine strainer. Flavor custard with orange and lemon rind and vanilla and almond extract.

Pour custard into 4-ounce molds. Place molds in a pan large enough to hold all of them. Pour hot water into pan until molds are half submerged in the water. Bake slowly at 325 degrees for 80 minutes. Cool; then chill molds. Remove custard from molds by running a skimming knife around the interior of the mold. Invert onto a dish, and shake gently.

Optional: Top with chopped nuts, preferably pistachio nuts, and/or fresh pressed berries.

Serves from sixteen to twenty.

Rice Pilaff

½ stick sweet butter
½ small onion, minced
2 cups converted rice
3 cups good chicken or fish stock
¼ teaspoon tarragon
Pinch of thyme
1 bay leaf

In a saucepan, sauté onion in butter until onion is wilted. Add rice, and stir constantly, being careful not to let rice pop and expand. Add herbs and chicken or **Fish Stock** (see page 116), and bring to a boil. Cover with a lid or aluminum foil. Bake in hot oven (500 degrees) for 18 to 20 minutes.

Serves eight.

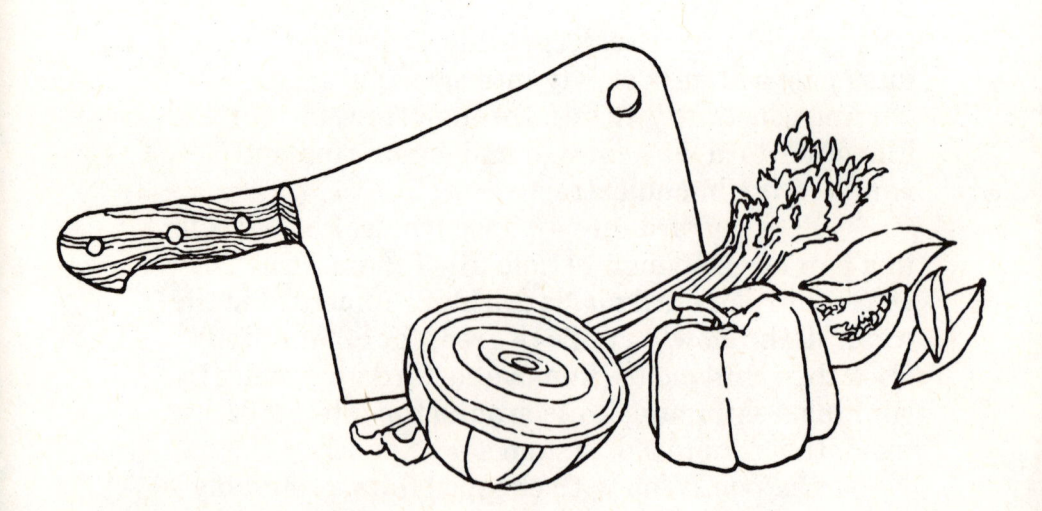

The Mandarin

900 North Point
Ghirardelli Square
San Francisco

Fillet of Rock Cod with Sweet and Sour Sauce

1 rock cod (about 3 pounds)
2 eggs
2 tablespoons water
Generous splash of sherry
2 heaping tablespoons all-purpose flour
Cornstarch
Cottonseed oil

Slice cod along backbone and below gills. Remove skin. Slice steaks lengthwise into strips, then crosswise into 2-inch segments. Make batter of eggs, water, sherry, and flour. Mix well. Dip cod into batter; then roll in cornstarch.

Heat oil over high temperature until bubbling. Deep fry cod 4 to 5 minutes until golden brown. Remove with strainer, and reserve.

Prepare **Sweet and Sour Sauce** (see recipe below). Refry fillets for 1 to 2 minutes. Drain, and place on platter. Pour sauce over fillets just before serving.

Serves four.

Sweet and Sour Sauce 1

1 cup sugar
1 cup water
½ cup white vinegar
4 tablespoons catsup
1 tablespoon soy sauce
2 tablespoons cornstarch in enough water to dissolve

Cook sugar, water, vinegar, and catsup over high heat for 2 to 3 minutes. Add soy sauce and cornstarch/water solution. Stir to blend and thicken.

Scallops Fu Yung

½ pound scallops
2 cups cottonseed oil
10 egg whites, lightly beaten until foamy
¼ pound bean sprouts
Chicken stock
3 to 4 scallions (white part only), shredded lengthwise
⅓ cup Virginia ham (or other uncooked ham), sliced thin and shredded
Pinch of sugar
Pinch of salt
Generous splash of sherry
Pinch of white pepper
Pinch of monosodium glutamate
Few drops of sesame oil
2 to 3 tablespoons cornstarch in enough water to dissolve
Fresh coriander (Chinese parsley)

Gently boil scallops for about 1 hour. Beat with whisk until shredded. Drain off liquid.

Heat oil in wok over medium temperature. Drop in egg whites, and turn off heat. When egg whites fluff up in oil, remove with a strainer. Reserve.

Using a strainer, simmer scallops and bean sprouts in chicken stock for 1 to 2 minutes. Drain.

Heat wok over high temperature. Coat inside surface with very little oil. Add scallions and ham. Toss and stir for 1 to 2 minutes. Then add scallops, bean sprouts, sugar, salt, sherry, white pepper, monosodium glutamate, sesame oil, and cornstarch/water solution, continuing to toss and stir.

Add egg whites. Toss and stir for 1 minute more. Garnish with coriander and serve.

Serves four.

Sweet and Sour Fish

1 rock cod, carp, or red snapper (about 3 pounds)
2 tablespoons soy sauce
2 tablespoons sherry
1 egg
4 tablespoons cornstarch
4 cups vegetable oil
Sweet pepper (optional)
Carrot shreds (optional)

Clean fish, leaving head, tail, and fins intact. Make five or six deep parallel slashes on both sides so sauce will soak into meat. Combine soy sauce, sherry, egg, and cornstarch. Rub mixture on both sides of fish.

Heat oil over high temperature until bubbling. Deep fry fish on both sides until deep golden brown. Remove fish to a long platter. The fish may be fried in advance and refried just before serving to make it crisper.

Prepare Sauce **Sweet and Sour** (see recipe below). Pour sauce over hot fish just before serving. Garnish with sweet pepper and carrot shreds, if desired.

Serves four.

Sweet and Sour Sauce 2

8 tablespoons catsup
4 tablespoons wine vinegar
8 tablespoons sugar
6 tablespoons soy sauce
4 tablespoons cornstarch, mixed with 2 cups water

Put catsup, vinegar, sugar, and soy sauce in a pot. Mix and boil for a few minutes. Gradually add cornstarch/water mixture, stirring until a thick sauce results.

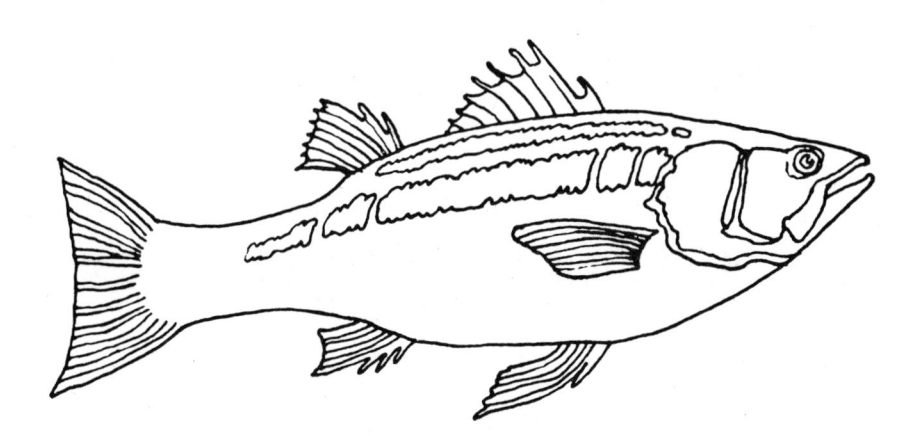

Modesto Lanzone's

900 North Point
Ghirardelli Square
San Francisco

Agnolotti

¼ pound finely ground raw veal and chicken meat
4 tablespoons finely ground prosciutto
1 chopped onion
3 tablespoons butter
½ cup dry white wine
½ teaspoon salt
⅛ teaspoon pepper
¼ cup grated Parmesan cheese

Prepare **Light White Sauce** (see recipe below). Prepare filling by mixing together all ingredients listed above. Prepare **Agnolotti Dough** (see recipe below). Roll thin. Cut in 3-inch squares. Place filling in center; fold dough over it at an angle, pressing edges together and curling sides to horseshoe shape. Boil filled pasta in salted water to taste. Serve agnolotti with white sauce.

Serves two.

Light White Sauce

½ pint whipping cream
2 tablespoons butter
⅛ teaspoon salt
⅛ teaspoon white pepper
2 drops of dry sherry

Bring mixture to light boil. Remove from fire. Add one egg yolk to sauce with fork to produce a light white sauce.

Agnolotti Dough

3½ cups sifted flour
3 eggs
1 tablespoon oil
1 teaspoon salt
1 egg, beaten with ½ teaspoon water to seal edges

Mix all ingredients together.

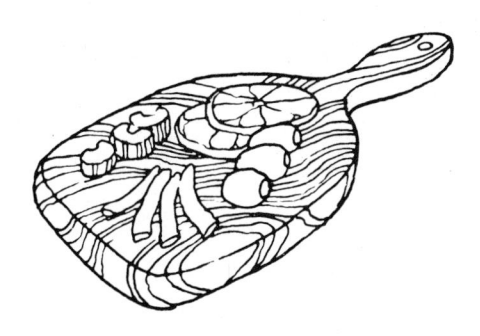

Scampi

24 large scampi, shelled
3 tablespoons oil
3 cloves garlic, chopped
6 sprigs parsley
Salt and white pepper to taste
1 cup dry white wine
½ lemon
½ cup butter (or more, as needed)

Place scampi in pan with oil over moderate heat. After 1 minute, place in hot oven for 1 or 2 minutes, depending on the size of the scampi. Remove from oven. Add garlic, parsley, salt and pepper and sauté. When garlic is brown, add wine and lemon. Reduce liquid to one-third. Add butter, strewing gently until butter melts. Pour sauce over scampi that has been placed on serving platter.

Serves six.

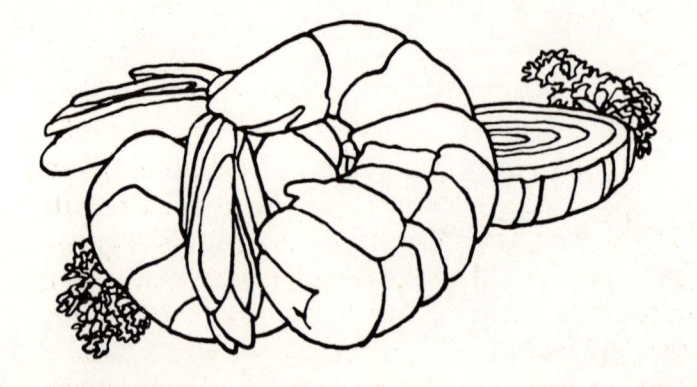

Restaurant Nakamura

Pier 39
San Francisco

Gyoza (Japanese Egg Roll)

1 pound ground pork
2 tablespoons fresh ginger, grated
3 leaves Napa cabbage, finely chopped after blanching
⅛ head cabbage, finely chopped
1 clove garlic, finely chopped
⅓ bunch leeks, finely chopped
⅛ cup soy sauce
Sprinkle of monosodium glutamate
3 tablespoons *sake*
1 teaspoon sesame chili oil
2 teaspoons sesame oil
3 tablespoons sugar
200 *gyoza* skins

Combine all *gyoza* ingredients except skins. Mix well with hands. Put one rounded teaspoon of mixture in each skin. Wet edges of skin, and fold over into decorative pattern. Heat frying pan to high heat; add 1 tablespoon vegetable oil to coat pan. Fry *gyoza* on flat side only until lightly brown (about 1 minute). Add enough hot water to cover *gyoza* halfway; cover, and reduce heat (to medium). After all water has evaporated (about 4 minutes or more), remove from heat. Serve hot with **Gyoza Dipping Sauce** (see recipe below). The *gyoza* can be frozen after they are made and before cooking.

Makes approximately 200 *gyoza*.

Gyoza Dipping Sauce

**One part vinegar
One part soy sauce
Chili oil to taste**

Combine ingredients together in a sauce bowl.

Teppan Yaki Sauces

These sauces may be used for dipping *teppan yaki* (steaks, chicken, pork, shellfish, and vegetables cooked at the table).

Ginger Sauce

**½ onion, chopped
6 tablespoons ginger, peeled and chopped
1 cup water
3 cups soy sauce
2 teaspoons** *sake*
Sprinkle of monosodium glutamate

Purée onion and ginger with water in a blender. In a bowl, combine the purée with soy sauce, *sake,* and monosodium glutamate. Stir well. Refrigerate. Stir before serving as needed for dipping.

Japanese Mustard Sauce

1 cup hot water, to make paste
¼ cup powdered mustard
¼ cup sesame seeds
3 cups soy sauce
2 teaspoons *sake*
Sprinkle of monosodium glutamate

Add enough hot water to mustard to make a thick paste. Let stand for 15 minutes. Toast sesame seeds in pan until brown; then grind seeds to coarse grains. Add other ingredients, and stir well. Refrigerate. Stir before serving as needed for dipping.

Nantucket Half Shell Restaurant

Pier 39
San Francisco

Nantucket Bay Scallops Sautéed

⅓ pound scallops per person
Flour, as needed
  3 sliced mushrooms
  3 tablespoons white wine
  3 tablespoons Fish Stock
  3 tablespoons raw butter
Salt to taste
Chopped parsley
Juice from a quarter of a lemon

Lightly flour scallops. Heat one-third of the butter in a saucepan and sauté scallops quickly on both sides until browned. Remove scallops from pan; then add mushrooms. Sauté until half cooked; add scallops and wine. Reduce heat. Add **Fish Stock** (see page 116), and cook until scallops are tender. Add the remaining butter. Season, sprinkle with parsley and lemon juice, and serve.

Serves one.

Neptune's Palace

Pier 39
San Francisco

Neptune's Palace Delight

1 pound cream cheese
¼ cup sugar
2 egg yolks
2 tablespoons brandy
¼ cup cream
Fresh fruit
Syrup
Fresh berries purée

    Whip cream cheese until nice and light. Add sugar, and cream well until sugar has been absorbed. Add egg yolks one at a time, beating thoroughly after each addition. Flavor with brandy. Mix well. Finish by whipping the cream and adding it to pudding. Blend well for several minutes. Chill for several hours.
    Using pastry bag, fill ramekin molds one-third full and chill. Top with fresh fruit in your favorite syrup or purée of fresh berries.
    Serves four.

Neptune's Palace Scallops Sauté with Snow Peas

8 or 9 plump scallops, well washed
Clarified butter
2 tablespoons sherry wine
¼ cup heavy cream
6 or 7 snow peas, washed
Salt, pepper, and nutmeg to taste
Fish Stock (optional)

Wash scallops well. Sauté scallops in butter for 2 minutes. Add sherry, stirring constantly. Do not let pan or scallops brown. Add cream, and reduce until sauce is thick and coats the back of a spoon. Add snow peas. Bring to a simmer; season with salt, pepper and nutmeg. Serve hot.

Serves one.

Optional: You may substitute a good **Fish Stock** (see page 116) with sherry already added to it, instead of using just sherry to give the sauce a bit more complexity in taste.

Old Swiss House

Pier 39
San Francisco

Pgules au Whiskey

8 pieces boneless chicken breast, sliced thin
½ cup butter
1 teaspoon mustard
Pinch of rosemary
2 tablespoons flour
2 tablespoons whiskey
2 tablespoons beef *jus*
1 cup heavy cream
Salt and pepper to taste
½ teaspoon Worcestershire sauce

    Sauté chicken in butter for 2 minutes. Add mustard, and mix. Season with a pinch of rosemary, and sprinkle with flour. Flame with whiskey. Add beef *jus* and heavy cream. Season with salt, pepper, and Worcestershire sauce. During the whole process, keep heat rather low.
    Serves four.

Pepe's On The Pier

Pier 39
San Francisco

Chile con Queso

3 cups milk
¾ pound grated Monterey Jack cheese
2 tablespoons minced onions
1 small clove garlic, minced
1 tablespoon butter
1 cup diced peeled tomatoes
¼ cup cornstarch
¼ cup chicken-base broth
⅛ cup diced fresh chile fresno
⅛ cup canned chili ortega
½ teaspoon crushed red hot pepper
Salt and ground white pepper to taste

In the upper half of a double boiler, heat the milk. Add the grated cheese, and set over low heat to melt. In a saucepan, sauté the onions and garlic in the butter until the onions are transparent. Add the tomatoes to the onions and garlic. Stir; then pour into the cheese mixture, stirring well. Put hot water in the bottom of the double boiler, and set over heat. Thicken the cheese mixture with the cornstarch mixed to a paste with chicken broth, stirring constantly. Add chopped chilies and other seasonings, and mix thoroughly. Set over hot water until ready to use. Pour into fondue pot, serve with corn chips.

Makes about 5 cups dip.

Hot Sauce Dip

2 cups fresh diced peeled tomatoes
3 cups diced onions
2 cups diced chile fresno
1 cup catsup
1½ tablespoons white vinegar
½ cup tomato juice
1½ teaspoons monosodium glutamate
1½ teaspoons minced garlic
1 cup chopped green pepper
1 cup chopped cilantro (Chinese parsley)
1 teaspoon whole oregano
1½ teaspoons white pepper
1½ tablespoons salt

Mix all ingredients together. Serve with corn chips.
Makes about 11 cups.

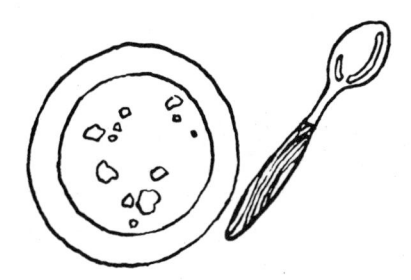

Rolf's Since 1960

757 Beach
San Francisco

Zwiebelfleisch (Grilled Tenderloin with Onions)

2 pounds beef tenderloin, sliced ¼ inch thick
2 cups thin-sliced onions
Salt and pepper to taste
½ cup clarified butter
½ cup oil
3 cups *soubise* (onion sauce)
1 cup sour cream
1 tablespoon finely chopped crisp bacon
1 tablespoon finely chopped parsley

Sauté meat. Set aside, and keep hot. Sauté onions until lightly brown in color. Place onions on top of meat. Pour off excess fat. Add *soubise* (see recipe below) to juices in pan. Bring to a boil; then lower heat and simmer. Add sour cream, salt and pepper, and simmer a little longer. Pour sauce over meat and onions. Garnish with bacon and parsley.
Serves six.

Soubise (Onion Sauce)

4 tablespoons flour
4 tablespoons butter
1 cup chicken broth
½ cup cream
½ cup onion purée
Salt and pepper to taste

Melt butter in a saucepan; add flour, and mix until well blended. Add broth and cream. Cook, stirring constantly. Now stir in **Onion Purée** (see recipe below). Season to taste.

Onion Purée

2 tablespoons butter
1 cup finely chopped onion

Steam onion in butter in a tightly covered saucepan until soft. Purée in blender.

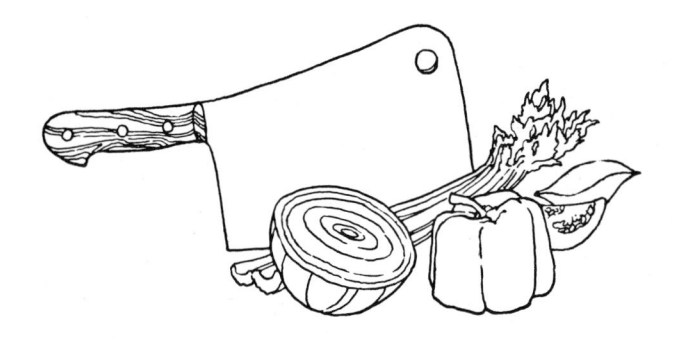

Rahm Schnitzel
(Veal Cutlets with Cream and Mushrooms)

2 pounds veal cutlets, sliced ¼ inch thick
1 cup lemon juice
Flour, as needed
4 tablespoons oil
1 cup sliced mushrooms
4 tablespoons butter, melted and clarified
½ cup Cream Sauce
½ cup cream
Salt and pepper to taste
Chablis wine

    Marinate veal in lemon juice in a stainless steel or glass dish. Pat dry, and roll in flour. Sauté meat in oil, and set it aside; keep warm. Sauté mushrooms in butter. Add **Cream Sauce** (see page 115) and cream. Season with salt and pepper. Bring to a boil, then simmer over low heat. Finish by adding a little Chablis wine. Pour sauce over cutlets, and serve.
    Serves five to six.

Paprika Schnitzel
(Veal Cutlets with Paprika)

2 pounds veal cutlets, sliced ¼ inch thick
1 cup lemon juice
Flour, as needed
4 tablespoons oil
1 cup sliced onions
Paprika to taste
4 tablespoons butter, melted and clarified
½ cup Cream Sauce
½ cup cream
Salt and pepper to taste

Marinate veal in lemon juice in a stainless steel or glass dish. Pat dry, and roll in flour. Sauté meat in oil, and set it aside; keep warm. Sauté onions in butter, and mix with paprika. Add **Cream Sauce** (see page 115) and cream. Season with salt and pepper. Bring to a boil. Then simmer over low heat. Pour sauce over cutlets, and serve.

Serves five to six.

The Rusty Scupper Restaurant

1800 Montgomery
San Francisco

Broiled Salmon Fillets with Hollandaise

6 10-ounce salmon fillets
Butter

    Broil salmon over grill, basting with butter before and after each turn. Serve **Hollandaise Sauce** (see page 115), with rice, a fresh vegetable, and lemon wedge.
    Serves six.

Scallops Morando

¼ pound butter
½ cup Chablis wine
2 pounds scallops
4 ounces fresh washed and stemmed spinach
4½ ounces sliced aged cheddar cheese (yellow)
16 drops of Worcestershire sauce
4 slices medium-sliced bacon
½ cup seasoned bread crumbs (sherry, butter, parsley flakes, paprika)

    Melt butter in a double boiler. Add wine. Heat slowly. When hot, add scallops. Poach for 10 minutes until approximately half cooked. Strain off broth.

Poach spinach separately, for 1½ minutes. Lightly coat four casserole dishes with butter. Add equal portions of scallops to each one. Dash four drops of Worcestershire into each dish. Cover scallops with equal portions spinach. Place slices of cheddar cheese over spinach. Cut each slice bacon into thirds; place over cheese. Sprinkle with seasoned bread crumbs. Bake for 7 to 10 minutes until bacon is done. Be careful not to burn cheese.

Serves four.

Chinese Shrimp Scampi

3 ounces carrots
3 ounces zucchini
2 teaspoons peanut oil
7 ounces peeled and deveined medium prawns
1 teaspoon soy sauce
½ teaspoon fresh garlic
¼ teaspoon fresh ginger
¼ teaspoon diced green onion
¼ teaspoon cilantro
1 teaspoon water

Boil carrots for 3 minutes. Cut carrots and zucchini into ¼-inch-thick sticks. Heat oil in a wok over a gas flame. When bubbling hot, add shrimp. Stir fry for approximately 45 seconds until cooked. Add soy sauce, garlic, ginger, green onions, and Chinese parsley. Stir well. Lower heat. Add water, carrots, and zucchini. Cover. Simmer for 2 minutes.

Serves one. Portions may be multiplied to serve up to three at one time.

A. Sabella's Restaurant

Fisherman's Wharf
San Francisco

Stuffed Turbot with Deviled Crab

2 medium mushrooms, sliced
1 clove garlic, crushed
1 chopped shallot
½ pimento, diced
½ teaspoon chopped parsley
1 tablespoon cooking oil
½ pound cooked crabmeat
1 tablespoon brandy
¼ cup sherry wine
½ cup Cream Sauce
1 well-beaten egg
Dash of hot sauce
4 drops Worcestershire sauce
Salt and pepper to taste
4 fillets of turbot
1 cup sherry wine
Salt to taste
Paprika
Drawn butter
Lemon slices

Sauté mushrooms, garlic, shallots, pimento and parsley in oil. Add crabmeat, brandy, 2 ounces sherry wine, **Cream Sauce** (see page 115), egg, hot sauce, and Worcestershire sauce. Season with salt and pepper. Mix together well. Cook for 10 minutes.

Place two fillets in a well-buttered baking pan. Put half of the crab mix on each fillet. Top each with another fillet. Press down firmly with hands, and lock with toothpicks so fillets will not come apart while cooking.

The turbot is now ready for the oven. Pour 1 cup sherry wine over turbot; sprinkle lightly with salt. Sprinkle with paprika. Pour melted butter over each turbot, and garnish with a slice of lemon. Bake in 400-degree oven for 20 to 25 minutes. Baste frequently.

Serves two.

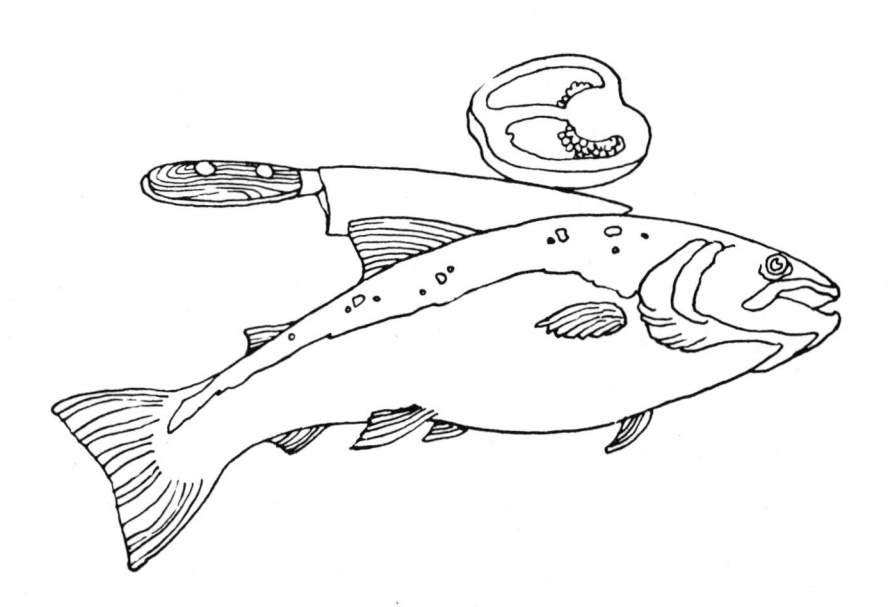

Crabmeat with Spaghetti

1 cup chopped onions
1 teaspoon chopped garlic
1 teaspoon chopped parsley
1 teaspoon chopped celery
4 tablespoons olive oil
1 cup solid-pack tomatoes
1½ cups water
2 teaspoons salt
1 teaspoon black pepper
1 pound fresh crabmeat
¼ cup sherry wine
1 pound spaghetti
½ teaspoon paprika
Grated Parmesan cheese

Sauté onions, garlic, parsley, and celery in olive oil until golden brown. Add solid-pack tomatoes, water, salt, and pepper. Simmer over low flame for 1 hour. Add crabmeat and wine, and simmer for another 10 minutes.

Cook and drain spaghetti. Place on platter. Pour sauce with crabmeat over spaghetti. Top with Parmesan cheese. Sprinkle with paprika. Serve hot.

Serves five.

Stuffed Swordfish Antone

2 center slices swordfish
½ cup chopped onions
1 tablespoon oil
1 cup shrimp
1 cup cooked chopped spinach
2 cups milk

Dash of cayenne
Pinch of dry mustard
½ teaspoon chopped parsley
1 tablespoon Worcestershire sauce
¼ cup sherry wine
Salt and pepper to taste
4 tablespoons flour
4 tablespoons melted butter
¼ cup chopped pimento

Sauté onion. Add shrimp and spinach. Cook 5 minutes. Add milk, then cayenne, mustard, parsley, Worcestershire sauce, and sherry wine. Bring to boil. Mix with salt, pepper, flour, and butter. Cook until thickened, stirring constantly.

Roll deviled shrimp inside two slices of swordfish. Bake 20 minutes.

Place in casserole. Cover with **Sauce Supreme** (see recipe below). Garnish with chopped pimento and grated cheese. Bake 20 minutes at 350 degrees.

Serves two.

Sauce Supreme

4 drops hot sauce
1 cup clam broth
2 tablespoons white wine

Add the above ingredients to basic white sauce.

Sabella and La Torre

Fisherman's Wharf
San Francisco

Crab Newburg Supreme

  2 tablespoons butter
  1 tablespoon minced onion
Green pepper
  1 tablespoon parsley
  1 cup sliced mushrooms
  2 tablespoons flour
1¾ cups milk
  ¼ cup sherry
  ½ teaspoon oregano
  ½ teaspoon thyme
Salt and pepper to taste
  2 cups crabmeat
  2 egg yolks

Melt butter in saucepan. Add onion, parsley, green pepper, and mushrooms. Cover, and cook gently for 10 minutes. Blend in flour, add milk, and continue cooking, stirring constantly, until mixture thickens. Add all other ingredients, and heat.

Serve in patty shells or on toast.

Serves two.

Shrimp Rarebit

5 tablespoons butter
7 tablespoons flour
2 cups milk
4 ounces shredded sharp cheddar cheese
1 tablespoon prepared mustard
1 level teaspoon salt
Pepper to taste
Dash of Worcestershire sauce
½ cup beer
Dash of cayenne
2 tablespoons mayonnaise
2 cups cooked shrimp

Melt butter, stir in flour, add milk and cheese. Cook, stirring constantly. Add all other ingredients except shrimp, and blend thoroughly. Add shrimp. Heat well.

Serve on buttered toast.

Serves two to four.

Prawns Patriced

4 stalks sliced celery
1 medium onion, sliced
1 large green pepper, sliced
1 clove garlic, minced
4 strips bacon, chopped
2 tablespoons olive oil
½ cup tomato purée
Juice of one lemon
2 pounds raw prawns, peeled
4 tomatoes, peeled and diced
Dash of hot sauce
1 tablespoon chopped parsley
2 tablespoons Worcestershire sauce
¼ cup sherry

Sauté celery, onion, pepper, garlic, and bacon in oil. Add tomato purée, lemon juice, and prawns, and simmer for 10 minutes. Add all other ingredients. Thicken slightly with cornstarch.

Serve with boiled or steamed rice.

Serves four.

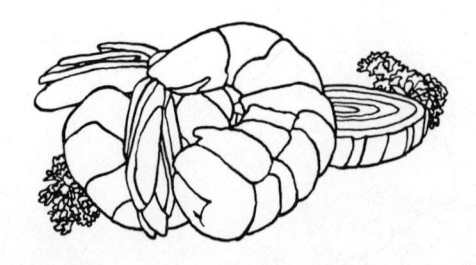

Salmon a l'Orlando

2-ounce can anchovy fillets
2 tablespoons olive oil
1 clove garlic, minced
¼ cup sherry wine
Chopped parsley
Juice of 1 lemon
2 pounds sliced salmon
Salt and pepper to taste

Drain oil from anchovies into pan. Add olive oil and garlic, and cook anchovies to a paste. Add wine, parsley, and lemon juice. Place salmon in baking pan; salt and pepper. Pour mixture over salmon. Bake about ½ hour at 400 degrees.

Serves four.

Sam's Grill and Seafood Restaurant

374 Bush
San Francisco

Clams Elizabeth

1 dozen medium clams
1 tablespoon finely chopped chives or scallions
2 tablespoons fine bread crumbs
1 tablespoon grated Parmesan cheese
Juice of 1 lemon
2 tablespoons melted butter
¼ cup sherry wine
Paprika

    Use any clams in season. Open each clam, leaving the clam in one half of the shell. Reserve the juice. Place the clams in a shallow dish. Pour a small amount of juice on each clam, and sprinkle with chives or scallions. Mix bread crumbs and cheese, and sprinkle lightly over each clam. Pour the lemon juice, then the butter, over all, and add the sherry wine around the edge. Cover lightly with paprika. Bake in a hot oven (400 degrees) for 20 minutes, or until brown.
    Serves one.

Deviled Crab ala Sam

6 stalks of celery, without leaves
2 medium onions
1 large green pepper
1½ cups vegetable oil
2 cups flour
Dash of ground white pepper
Dash of ground nutmeg
3 teaspoons dry mustard
1½ quarts scalded milk
2 pounds fresh crabmeat
Grated Parmesan cheese
Dash of paprika
Melted butter

Chop celery, onions, and green pepper very fine. Cook slowly in oil until tender (about 10 minutes). Stirring constantly, sprinkle and add flour, white pepper, nutmeg, and mustard. Keep stirring until smooth and bubbling. Still stirring constantly, add hot scalded milk; continue stirring fast till sauce is thick and smooth. Add crabmeat. (If you use canned crabmeat, drain off all juice before adding to sauce.) Stir well, and cook until it starts to boil; remove from fire. Heat oven to 400 degrees. Pour crab with sauce into ovenproof casserole or serving dish. Sprinkle generously with Parmesan cheese, add a dash of paprika, and dribble with melted butter. Bake in oven until golden brown (about 5 minutes).
Serves four.

Hangtown Fry

25 to 30 baby oysters
Flour
Eggwash (1 beaten egg with 1 teaspoon milk)
Bread crumbs
Oil for deep frying
  2 tablespoons butter or margarine
  2 or 3 eggs
  2 slices bacon

Roll oysters in flour, so they are well coated. Dip into eggwash; then roll in fine bread crumbs. Deep fry in oil; drain and put aside.

Melt butter in frying pan; whip the eggs, and pour into frying pan. Stir slightly, and add prepared oysters while eggs are still half done so that they will bind the oysters. Flip omelette, and cook on other side. In the meantime, cook bacon in second pan. When omelette and bacon are done (it should be at the same time), slip the omelette onto platter and top with the cooked bacon. Serve immediately.

Serves one.

Scoma's

Pier 47
Fisherman's Wharf
San Francisco

Sole Fish ala Via Reggio

½ medium onion, chopped
1 clove garlic, minced
Sliced fresh mushrooms
Pinch oregano
½ cup white wine
2 or 3 tablespoons solid-pack tomatoes, ground
1 tablespoon tomato paste
1 cup water
1 pound sole
Chopped fresh spinach
Salt and pepper to taste

Sauté onion, garlic, and mushrooms in small amount of oil until onion turns golden. Add oregano, wine, tomatoes, tomato paste, and water. Cook this sauce for 5 minutes. Add sole. Cook over low heat for 15 minutes. A few minutes before fish is cooked, add chopped fresh spinach. Season.

Serves two.

Canneloni (with Seafood Filling)

½ medium onion, chopped
½ clove garlic, chopped
Sliced fresh mushrooms
Oil
 1 tablespoon white wine
 1 cup Supreme Sauce
½ pound crabmeat
½ pound shrimp meat
Parmesan cheese
Sliced Monterey jack cheese

Prepare **Napolitana Sauce** (see recipe below). As it simmers, prepare **Supreme Sauce** (see recipe below). Set aside.

Sauté onion, garlic, and mushrooms in a small amount of oil. Add wine, Supreme Sauce, crab, shrimp, and a pinch of Parmesan cheese. Stir. Allow filling to cool.

Prepare crepe batter (using any standard recipe). In a lightly greased pan, cook 1 tablespoon of batter for 1 minute on each side. Place 1 tablespoon of filling on each crepe. Roll.

In a large baking pan, put ½ cup Napolitana Sauce. Place the filled canneloni in the pan. Put in preheated, 350-degree oven for 3 to 4 minutes. Remove pan from oven. Top each canneloni with a pinch of Parmesan cheese and a slice of Monterey jack cheese.

Return pan to oven. The canneloni are ready to serve when the cheese topping has melted.

Serves four.

Napolitana Sauce

1 medium onion, chopped
4 cloves garlic, chopped
Oil
Pinch of oregano
3 to 4 bay leaves
1 no. 10 can solid-pack tomatoes, ground
1 tablespoon tomato paste
1 cup water
Salt to taste
Pinch of chili pepper
Sugar, as needed

Sauté onion and garlic in oil. Season with oregano and bay leaves. When onion turns golden, add tomatoes, tomato paste, and water. Simmer for ½ hour. Add sugar to reduce acidity.

Supreme Sauce

1 cup butter
1 cup flour
6 cups hot milk

Melt butter in a pan. Blend in flour, stirring over low heat (all flour must be blended with the butter for a smooth sauce).
Stir in the milk. Season with salt. Cook for approximately 3 minutes, stirring so the sauce is smooth.

Abalone Bordelaise

1 pound abalone
Flour
2 or 3 beaten eggs
1 cup oil

    Dip abalone in flour and then in eggs. Heat oil in a frying pan until it is hot. Fry abalone for approximately 1 minute on each side.
    Pour **Bordelaise Sauce** (see recipe below) over it. Serve.
    Serves two to three.

Bordelaise Sauce

½ medium onion, chopped fine
1 clove garlic, minced
1 tablespoon white wine
½ cup Supreme Sauce
Lemon juice

    Sauté onion and garlic in a little oil until onion turns golden. Squeeze lemon juice over the onion and garlic. Add wine and **Supreme Sauce** (see recipe on page 77). Stir over low heat.

Scott's Seafood Grill and Bar

3 Embarcadero Center
2400 Lombard
San Francisco

Broiled Salmon

Select a nice pink salmon fillet with a firm texture. Preheat the broiler section of the oven. Brush the fillet with oil or melted butter, season with salt and pepper, and place on broiler pan. Broil under broiler flame for 4 to 5 minutes on each side. Allow 10 minutes cooking time per inch of thickness of fillet.

If salmon fillets are too thick, broil on both sides, then place on well-greased pan with some water or fish stock and continue cooking in moderate oven. Remove salmon skin. Serve immediately with **Hollandaise Sauce** (see page 115).

Fisherman's Stew

2 medium carrots
1 large leek
2 stalks celery
¼ pound mushrooms
2-3 medium cloves garlic, finely chopped
½ pound prawns, peeled and deveined
½ pound scallops (cut in ½ if using large sea scallops)
1 pound thick fish fillet (such as rock cod), cut into 1-inch-thick cubes
8 cherrystone clams, washed and opened

**2 quarts Fish Stock
1 cup white wine
4 ounces bay shrimp
4 ounces crabmeat
8 ounces whole butter
2 lemons, cut into crowns
Chopped parsley**

Prepare in individual stew pots or one large pot. If serving in individual stew pots, divide the ingredients by four, and place proper amount in each pot.

Wash and slice vegetables to ¼ inch thick. Place them in stew pot along with garlic, prawns, scallops, fish fillets, clams, **Fish Stock** (see page 116), and wine. Cover, and bring to a boil. Reduce heat. Simmer gently until fish is just cooked (about 6 minutes). Add crabmeat, shrimp, and butter. Continue to simmer until the crab and shrimp are heated through and the butter is melted.

Note: If using one large pot, heat shrimp and crab separately in some fish stock and white wine, and portion into individual serving bowls as garnish.

Garnish with ½ lemon cut into a crown and dusted in chopped parsley. Serve immediately.

Serves four.

Sea of Cortez

Pier 39
San Francisco

Clam Chowder

½ cup diced salt pork
1 large onion, diced
¾ cup diced celery
Flour
Clam liquor drained from clams
2 cups soup stock
2 cups light cream or half-and-half
2 large potatoes, parboiled and diced
½ tablespoon thyme
¼ cup chopped parsley
1½ cups chopped clams

Fry out salt pork; remove pork from pan and save. In the same frying pan, sauté onions and celery until half cooked. Then add enough flour to make a soft *roux*. Add clam liquor, soup stock, cream, potatoes, salt pork, thyme, and parsley. Bring to a boil; then simmer for 10 minutes. Add chopped clams last, as they do not require much cooking. Season, and serve.

Serves four.

Bouillabaisse

10 ounces tomato sauce
¾ cup clam juice
6 tablespoons chopped clams
2 teaspoons thyme
1½ teaspoons oregano
Pinch of salt
2 pinches of white pepper
1 cup large diced celery
½ cup large diced onion
1 clove garlic, minced
½ cup butter
1½ pounds whitefish
Flour
Butter
1½ cups white wine
¼ cup sherry
3 or 4 Littleneck clams per person, in shell

In a large soup pot, combine tomato sauce, clam juice, chopped clams, thyme, oregano, salt, and pepper. Simmer.

In another pan, sauté celery, onion, and minced garlic in butter.

Dust whitefish in flour. Sauté in butter until half cooked. Add white wine and sherry. Poach fish in liquid just until fish flakes separate easily when gently probed with a fork.

Combine vegetables and poached fish in soup pot; add clams. Simmer bouillabaisse until clams open.

Serves four to six.

Shang Yuen Restaurant

600 Beach
The Cannery
San Francisco

Prawns a la Szechwan

12 prawns (about 1⅓ pounds)
6 cups oil
1 tablespoon chopped garlic
1 tablespoon chopped ginger root
½ teaspoon chopped dried red chili peppers (optional)
1 tablespoon chopped onion
1 tablespoon fermented rice wine (or cooking wine)
4 tablespoons tomato catsup
½ teaspoon salt
1 tablespoon sugar
1 teaspoon monosodium glutamate
3 tablespoons water
1 teaspoon cornstarch

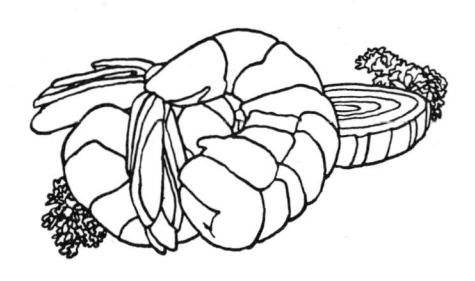

Cut antennae and other appendages from prawns; rinse and devein; drain.

Heat oil. When hot, deep fry prawns for 2 minutes over high heat; remove, and drain. Remove all but 2 tablespoons of oil from pan.

Reheat and stir fry garlic, ginger, chili peppers (if desired), and onion until fragrant. Add wine and catsup, and stir fry ½ minute. Add prawns, salt, sugar, monosodium glutamate, water, and cornstarch. When mixture begins to boil, add 1 tablespoon oil, and toss lightly to mix ingredients and coat prawns with sauce. Remove and portion onto plates. Serve.

Serves two.

Shipboard Restaurant Sailing Ship *Dolphin P. Rempp*

Pier 42
San Francisco

Shrimp Paulette

1 pound jumbo shrimp, cooked and peeled
1 cup thinly sliced onions, 1 inch long
½ cup butter or margarine
1 cup thinly sliced celery, 1 inch long
2 cups whole fresh mushrooms
1 cup thinly sliced green peppers, 1 inch long
¼ cup sliced pimentos, ½ inch long
1 teaspoon chopped garlic
4 cups Cream Sauce (or canned cream of mushroom soup)
¼ cup white wine
¼ cup mixed green onions and parsley
Salt and pepper to taste

Slice shrimp almost in half the flat way. Sauté shrimp and onions in butter with lid on. Add celery, mushrooms, peppers, pimentos, and garlic. Cook 3 minutes. Add **Cream Sauce** (see page 115). Cook 5 minutes with lid on. Add wine; stir. Add green onions and parsley. Taste, and correct with salt and pepper. (If too thick, add 1 cup milk, cook 1 minute, and stir.) Serve over rice.

Serves four.

Stradel's Fish Grotto

Fisherman's Wharf
San Francisco

Sweet and Sour Salmon Steaks

1 cup flour
4 salmon steaks
½ cup oil
2 or 3 diced onions
1 teaspoon thyme
Salt and pepper to taste
⅓ cup red wine vinegar

Flour salmon steaks on both sides. Put oil in frying pan; when hot, brown steaks on both sides. Lay steaks on platter. To the same frying pan, add diced onions. Brown well; then add thyme, salt and pepper, and wine vinegar. Cook for 1 minute more. Pour sauce over salmon steaks. Serve.
Serves four.

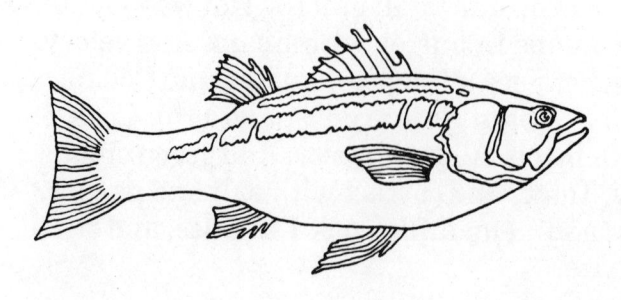

Fried Sand Dabs

8 sand dabs
Salt and pepper to taste
2 cups flour
1 cup cooking oil

Clean fish; wash and dry. Season with salt and pepper, and roll in flour. Heat oil in pan. Fry sand dabs until browned well on both sides; remove. Place on platter. Top with lemon slices. Serve.
Serves four.

Fried Abalone Steak

4 abalone steaks
Salt and pepper to taste
1 or 2 beaten eggs
1½ cups fine bread crumbs
1 cup oil
1 tablespoon chopped parsley
1 quarter of a lemon

Abalone already prepared for cooking may be purchased from dealer. Wipe dry. Season with salt and pepper. Dip abalone in beaten egg, then in bread crumbs. Heat oil over moderate fire. When quite hot, put abalone in pan. Care must be taken that pan does not become too hot. Fry only until browned slightly on both sides. If cooked too long, it will become chewy. Place on platter. Garnish with parsley, and top with lemon. Serve with **Tartar Sauce** (see page 117).
Serves four.

Swiss Louis Restaurant

Pier 39
San Francisco

Frittata a la Louis

4 tablespoons butter
1 finely chopped white onion
½ bell pepper, finely chopped
9 beaten eggs
6 ounces finely chopped cooked spinach
½ cup Parmesan cheese
Salt and pepper to taste
8 ounces finely chopped ham

Melt butter in frying pan over medium flame. Add onion and bell pepper; brown lightly. Add mixture of eggs, spinach, cheese, ham, and salt and pepper. Cover, and cook for 2 to 3 minutes, or more if needed. Remove from pan. Cut into quarters. Serve.
Serves four.

Rex Sole Meunière with Capers

4 Rex sole

Clean and flour sole. Grill over low heat. Place two Rex sole in each dish. Pour over **Meunière Sauce** (see recipe below). Top with chopped parsley, and serve.

Serves two.

Meunière Sauce

4 tablespoons butter
Juice of 1 lemon
½ cup white wine
1 tablespoon vinegar
1 tablespoon capers
Sprig of parsley, finely chopped
Salt, pepper, and monosodium glutamate to taste

Melt butter in frying pan over very hot flame. Add lemon juice, wine, vinegar, and capers. Add salt, pepper, and monosodium glutamate when all ingredients are hot.

Pesto Sauce

2 cups fresh basil leaves
¼ cup fresh parsley
1 cup pine nuts or walnuts
2 cloves garlic, chopped fine
Monosodium glutamate to taste
Salt to taste
3 cups olive oil
Muffin paper cups

Finely grind basil, parsley, nuts, garlic, and oil. Then mix salt and monosodium glutamate. Fill muffin cups ¾ full, and freeze mixture. When partially frozen, pour oil to top of paper cup and freeze. Leave in freezer until ready to use.
Use over hot noodles or pasta.

Tripe

2 pounds tripe
2 lemons, quartered

Boil tripe with lemons for 1½ hours. Run hot water over tripe to get fat off. Then run cool water over tripe. Cut into ½-inch-by-2-inch strips. Make **Tomato Sauce** (see recipe below). Add tripe to sauce with potatoes, and cook until potatoes are tender.
Serves four.

Tomato Sauce

4 tablespoons butter
1 finely chopped onion
2 stalks celery, finely chopped
1 clove garlic, finely chopped
1 14-ounce can solid-pack tomatoes
1¾ cups water
1 tablespoon salt pork
1 cup beef broth
1 cup white wine
Salt and pepper to taste
2 diced potatoes
Monosodium glutamate to taste

Melt butter in frying pan over medium flame. Add onions, celery, and garlic. Brown lightly. Add tomatoes, water, salt pork, salt and pepper, and monosodium glutamate. Simmer for 10 minutes. Then add broth and wine, and simmer for ½ hour. Add potatoes, and cook until they are tender.

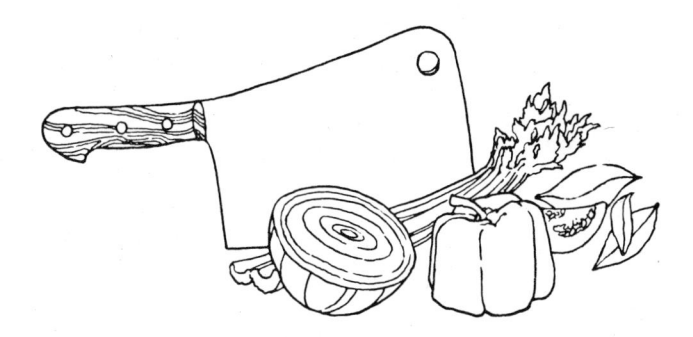

Wild Duck

1 wild duck
1 celery stalk
1 apple
1 tablespoon oil
¼ cup white wine
4 tablespoons butter
Salt and pepper to taste
1 teaspoon lemon juice
1 teaspoon A-1 sauce
1 teaspoon catsup
1 shot brandy
1 shot Kirsch Crème de Almond
½ teaspoon chopped parsley

Stuff wild duck with chunks of celery and apples. Bake at 550 degrees for 15 minutes. Remove from oven, and quickly carve the breast out. Put the breast in skillet with a little oil. Fry 30 seconds on each side. Add white wine.

In a large skillet, place butter, salt and pepper, lemon juice, A-1 sauce, catsup, brandy, and Kirsch Crème de Almond. Keep stirring until sauce is hot. The sauce should be tangy and not too sweet. Put duck breast on plate. Pour sauce over duck. Top with parsley.

Serves two.

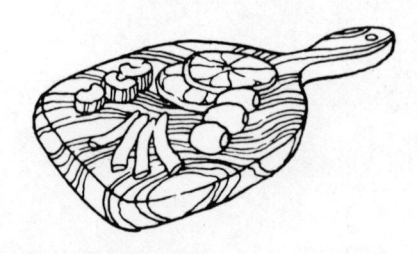

Tarantino's Restaurant

206 Jefferson
Fisherman's Wharf
San Francisco

Crab and Turbot

½ cup Cream Sauce
1 tablespoon Worcestershire sauce
2 tablespoons dry mustard
3 tablespoons French mustard
½ teaspoon chopped shallots
¼ cup chopped pimentos
4 chopped hardboiled eggs
1 pound crabmeat
Salt and pepper to taste
8 slices turbot or fillet of sole

Make **Cream Sauce** (see page 115) of medium thickness, and bring to a boil. Add Worcestershire sauce, both mustards, a little at a time, shallots, pimentos, eggs, crabmeat, and salt and pepper to taste.

Place the turbot slices in a buttered casserole. Pour sauce and crabmeat over fish. Bake in 400-degree oven for 20 to 25 minutes.

Serves four.

Tarantino's Lazy Man's Cioppino

1 pound crabmeat
6 large shrimp, cooked
10 Eastern oysters
10 clams, if available

Place in **Cioppino Sauce** (see recipe below). Simmer for 10 minutes. Serve in casserole or deep dish with hot, buttered garlic toast.

Serves five.

Cioppino Sauce

¼ pound butter
6 finely chopped leeks
3 finely chopped onions
3 finely chopped green peppers
6 stalks celery, chopped fine
1 tablespoon finely chopped garlic
¼ teaspoon whole thyme
¼ teaspoon rosemary
1 cup dry white wine
1 no. 10 can solid-pack tomatoes
1 quart water
Salt and pepper to taste

Sauté in butter (but do not brown) the finely chopped vegetables and spices.

Add tomatoes, wine, and water, and salt and pepper to vegetables. Cook until reduced one quarter.

Tokyo Sukiyaki

225 Jefferson
Fisherman's Wharf
San Francisco

Teriyaki

Teriyaki is broiled pieces of marinated meat or shellfish.

Teriyaki Sauce

1 cup Japanese soy sauce
3 tablespoons granulated sugar
½ cup Mirin (sweet rice wine)
1 teaspoon monosodium glutamate

Mix all ingredients together.

Sukiyaki

1 large piece beef suet (fat)
1 pound beef (boned prime rib, sliced one-eighth inch thick in reasonable-sized pieces)
1 bunch fresh green onions (cut in 2-inch lengths)
1 piece onion
4 medium-sized fresh mushrooms, sliced
¼ piece *tofu* (soy bean cake), cut into pieces approximately 1-by-1½-inches
¼ pound *shirataki* (fine vermicelli-like threads of gelatinous starch)
1 piece bamboo shoot
2 medium-sized eggs

     Prepare **Sukiyaki Sauce** (see recipe below). Set aside.
     Place a heavy, shallow saucepan on the fire. Allow it to heat up. Place beef suet in pan to grease it well. Take out used fat.
     Spread slices of beef on the sizzling pan. Brown slightly to rare. Add onions, vegetables, mushrooms, *tofu, shirataki,* and bamboo shoot in that order. (Theoretically, the longer-to-cook ingredients are placed in the pan first.)
     Quickly add Sukiyaki Sauce (use additional sugar to suit the taste.) When the host is adept in cooking sukiyaki, no other liquid need be used, since the water content of the vegetables produces enough moisture. However, if while cooking, the pan becomes too dry, add reasonable amounts of broth to make a light cooking sauce.
     Cook for a few minutes, and the sukiyaki is ready. Sukiyaki may be dipped in a beaten raw egg to cool it before eating.

Sukiyaki Sauce 1

½ cup Japanese soy sauce
2 tablespoons granulated sugar
4 tablespoons *sake*
½ cup beef broth

Mix all ingredients together.

Sukiyaki Sauce 2

5 cups beef broth
2 cups Japanese soy sauce
3 tablespoons granulated sugar
½ cup *sake*
3 tablespoons monosodium glutamate

Mix all ingredients together.

Tempura

Tempura is deep-fried, batter-coated pieces of seafood or vegetables.

Fill skillet with vegetable oil 2 inches deep. Set temperature control at 350 degrees. Dip vegetable pieces or seafood bits individually into **Tempura Batter** (see recipe below) and then in hot oil. Time for cooking depends on each ingredient.

Ingredients should be removed just before they are thoroughly cooked. Serve with **Tempura Sauce** (see recipe below).

Tempura Batter

1 egg
½ cup water
1 cup flour

Beat egg well. Add water and flour. Stir lightly.

Tempura Sauce

5 cups bonito soup
1 cup Japanese soy sauce
½ cup *sake*
5 tablespoons granulated sugar
1 tablespoon monosodium glutamate

Mix all ingredients together.

Vannelli's Seafood

Pier 39
San Francisco

Vannelli's Fisherman's Stew

1 large diced onion
1 cup mushrooms, cut into quarters
1 cup diced celery
1 tablespoon chopped parsley
1 level tablespoon finely chopped shallots
2 cups burgundy wine
½ cup melted butter
1 cup diced tomatoes
4 cloves garlic, finely chopped
Bay leaf, thyme, salt, black pepper, and cayenne pepper to taste
16 clams
32 prawns (21 to 24 per pound)
8 medium-sized scallops
8 calamari, cleaned, cut, and parboiled
4 ounces salmon, cut into 1-ounce cubes
4 ounces halibut, cut into 1-ounce cubes
Fish Stock or water

Wilt all vegetables in butter. Add tomatoes and herbs and seasonings. Then add all the fish, wine, and enough **Fish Stock** (see page 116) or water to cover all ingredients. Bring to a boil over low heat. Simmer for 10 minutes. Serve with garlic bread.
Serves four.

The Waterfront Restaurant

Pier 7
San Francisco

Thrasher Shark, Sautéed and Capered

Cooking oil
24 ounces thrasher shark
Salt and white pepper to taste
½ cup white wine
3 tablespoons capers
3 tablespoons caper vinegar
Butter, to taste
Chopped parsley

    Heat cooking oil, and sauté shark about 3 minutes on each side, or until fish flakes separate easily when gently probed with a fork. Salt and pepper both sides of fish. Pour off oil; add white wine, capers, caper vinegar, butter, and parsley. Heat and serve.
    Serves four.

California Rock Cod

24 ounces rock cod fillets
Salt and pepper to taste
Flour, as needed
  1 mashed avocado
Lemon juice
Teleme cheese, sliced

      Season fillets with salt and pepper. Dust with flour. Sauté lightly in oil until cooked through and browned (approximately 4 minutes). Season mashed avocado with salt, pepper, and lemon juice. Spread cooked fish with avocado. Top with slices of cheese. Place under the broiler until cheese is melted.
      Serves four.

Crayfish

  1 stalk celery
  1 carrot
  1 onion
½ clove garlic
48 crayfish
Mustard, mayonnaise, lettuce
½ lemon, sliced

      Bring vegetables to a boil in a gallon of water. Boil 15 minutes. Add crayfish, and bring to a second boil. Boil 3 minutes or until red. Remove crayfish. Cool in ice water. Serve on a bed of lettuce with mustard, mayonnaise, and lemon slices.
      Serves four.

White Whale Restaurant

900 North Point
Ghirardelli Square
San Francisco

White Whale Papillote

4 ounces butter
8 green onions (scallions), sliced very fine
2 pounds fillet of sole or cod
6 ounces finely sliced fresh-cooked shrimp
12 ounces white crabmeat
Salt and pepper to taste
½ cup dry white wine
¼ cup sherry wine
1½ pints Fish Velouté or Cream Sauce
Few dashes hot pepper sauce

In a shallow saucepan, melt butter. Place the sliced green onions and the fish in it. Over and around it, place the sliced shrimp and fresh white crabmeat. Cover, and let simmer or steam for a few minutes. At that time, sprinkle with salt and pepper; moisten with white wine and sherry wine. Cover again, and cook over low heat until fish is done and firm.

Carefully remove fish from saucepan. Reserve in a warm place while completing the sauce.

To the shrimp, crabmeat and juices in saucepan add **Fish Velouté** (see recipe below) or **Cream Sauce** (see page 115). Bring to a fast boil while stirring. Rectify the seasoning, and add a few dashes of hot pepper sauce (taste must be very sharp). Then proceed as follows.

Cut special white parchment paper in a heart-shaped piece about 14 inches across at its widest point. Oil the outside of the paper. Lay the oiled side flat on table. In center of right side of heart, place 2 teaspoons of sauce as prepared above; on it, lay the cooked fish. Then cover it with 2 teaspoons of sauce.

To close the paper bag, fold over the left half of paper on the fish. Roll edges of paper, starting from the left inside top of the shape. Continue with small, even turns until envelope is firmly closed all around to the very tip of the heart shape. Turn in paper point to hold shape. Place the bag on folded side on a well-oiled baking pan. Place pan on top of range for a few minutes, or until bag begins to puff. Then place pan in a very hot oven until paper bag is browned. Slide from pan onto plate. Serve.

At the table, supply a very sharp, pointed knife to cut paper. Lift paper, and uncover one of the most delicious fish dishes that could be prepared.

Serves six.

Fish Velouté

2 tablespooons butter
2 tablespoons flour
1 cup Fish Stock
Salt and pepper to taste

Combine butter and flour; stir in **Fish Stock** (see page 116) gradually, and heat to a boil. Cook until thickened, stirring occasionally. Add salt and pepper.

Makes 1 cup.

Yet Wah Mandarin Cuisine

Pier 39
San Francisco

Lemon Chicken Yet Wah Style

2 whole chicken breasts, skinned and boned
1 teaspoon oil
1 teaspoon cornstarch
2 tablespoons oil
½ teaspoon salt
1 teaspoon soy sauce
1 celery stalk, cut diagonally in 1-inch sections
½ green pepper, seeded and cut in ½-inch squares
½ red pepper, seeded and cut in ½-inch squares
1 carrot, peeled and cut diagonally in ¼-inch slices
2 tablespoons green peas
4 red maraschino cherries, halved
1 teaspoon lemon juice
¼ teaspoon sugar
¼ teaspoon monosodium glutamate (optional)
½ cup pineapple-orange juice
4 slices lemon
2 teaspoons cornstarch
1 tablespoon water

Cut chicken into 1-inch squares. Mix together with 1 teaspoon oil and cornstarch. Allow chicken to marinate in this mixture while you prepare the other ingredients (or for at least 15 minutes).

Place skillet or wok over high heat. When pan is hot, add 2 tablespoons oil. Add the chicken, salt, and soy sauce. Stir fry for 1 minute. Add the vegetables, cherries, lemon juice, sugar, monosodium glutamate, pineapple-orange juice, and lemon slices. Cover the pan. Cook over medium heat for 2 minutes.

Blend cornstarch and water to form a paste, and stir in to thicken the sauce.

Serves four as a main course, or six to eight as part of a complete Chinese meal.

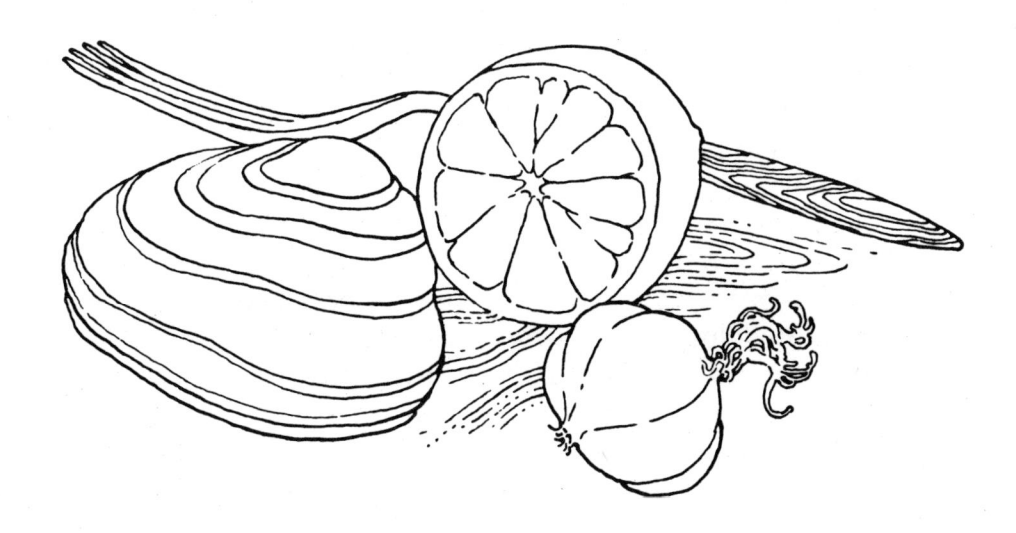

Yet Wah Special Lamb

⅔ pound boned shoulder or leg of lamb, cut in ⅛-inch diagonal slices
2 teaspoons cornstarch
2 tablespoons oil
¼ cup shredded carrots
¼ cup bamboo shoots
3 green onions, sliced
½ cup shredded Chinese cabbage
½ teaspoon salt
½ teaspoon sugar
Rice stick noodles
1 sliced green onion

Sprinkle lamb with cornstarch, and rub into the meat. Prepare **Yet Wah Special Lamb Sauce** (see recipe below), and place it near the stove. Place wok or skillet over high heat; when very hot, add 1 tablespoon oil. Add carrots, bamboo shoots, green onions, Chinese cabbage, salt, and sugar. Stir fry for 3 minutes, and remove to a plate.

Pour remaining tablespoon of oil into wok or skillet. Add lamb. Stir fry for 2 minutes, add sauce, and cook for a minute longer. Return vegetables to the wok, and cook briefly to heat vegetables through.

Serve Yet Wah Special Lamb on a bed of rice stick noodles, briefly deep fried in hot oil and removed with a slotted spoon. Place the Yet Wah Special Lamb on the crisp noodles. Garnish with slivered green onions.

Serves two as a main course, or four to six as part of a complete Chinese meal.

Yet Wah Special Lamb Sauce

¼ teaspoon salt
¼ teaspoon monosodium glutamate (optional)
¼ teaspoon sugar
½ teaspoon soy sauce
½ teaspoon cornstarch
2 teaspoons Hoisin sauce
1 teaspoon plum sauce
1 teaspoon tomato sauce
½ teaspoon oyster sauce

Mix all ingredients together.

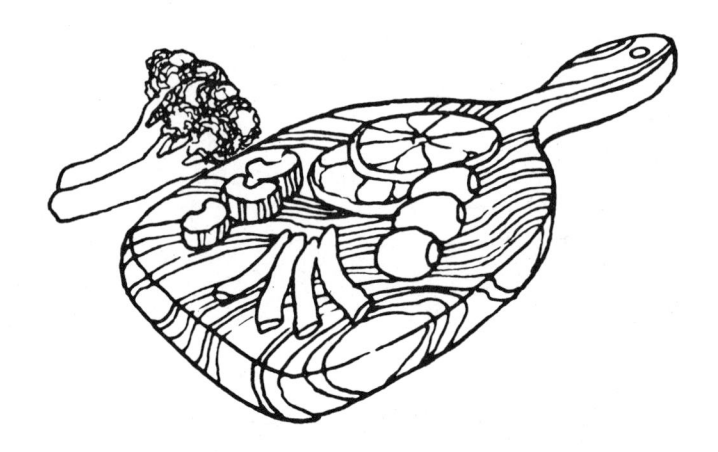

Dalmatian Fish Cookery

The Dalmatian tradition of fish cookery, born along the coast of the Adriatic Sea in Yugoslavia, has been to obtain fish that is almost flopping fresh, then cook it precisely to that evasive instant which barely divides unappetizing translucency from desiccation — and to cook it relatively plainly.

What you then taste, be it sole, salmon, or sea bass, is a flaky flesh with a delicate flavor. There is never a sauce or herb so strong that it covers up the natural flavor — just a sprinkling of parsley and perhaps a bit of lemon and butter.

Sounds ordinary? Just try to achieve that kind of sensitivity at home!

In the waning decades of the Austro-Hungarian empire, while fighting the Turks, the Hapsburg reign exploited what is now Yugoslavia through taxation and conscription. Under such pressures, inhabitants of the agriculturally impoverished Dalmatian coast suffered deprivation. Hence the great migration of the nineteenth and twentieth centuries.

Many of the Dalmatians had been fishermen, so it was natural for them to follow the same occupation once they reached America or to establish restaurants serving fish, the principal source of protein in the old country.

If they failed to call their restaurants Yugoslavian, this lapse was easily explained, since the nation of that name did not come into existence until the end of World War I, in 1918. Indeed, the restaurateurs seemed to go out of their way to take on an American image. While serving up blue-plate specials and merchant lunches, the Dalmatians may have failed to realize the extent of their own contribution.

Because their soil was unproductive, the Dalmatians were obliged to seek their food from the sea. The Dalmatian was more of a seafarer than even the neighboring Italian. The Yugoslavian coastline has many islands and inlets which historically have provided harbors of refuge against Adriatic storms — harbors the Italian coast lacks.

The catch was so precious, moreover, that people prepared it with utmost care. "Care" in this context means a caution against overcooking, which deprives fish of texture as well as taste.

The traditional methods of cooking the fish were plain ones such as charcoal broiling (*gradele*) and poaching. With their proximity to the Adriatic, the Dalmatians were able to feast on fish so fresh that they had no reason to disguise it with sauces or seasonings.

In San Francisco, the Dalmatians established their predominance in catching. Historian Adam S. Eterovich believes that more than two hundred and fifty Dalmatian fishermen lived in San Francisco in the 1870s. According to the California Historical Society, the Fisherman's Wharf Protective Association was headed by a Dalmatian in 1877, 1881, and again in 1884.

Four major fish restaurants in San Francisco (and various chefs in the kitchens of others) have carried on the Dalmatian tradition. At Tadich's (240 California Street), John V. Tadich, a native of Starigrad, took on a second cook, Dominic Ivelich, in 1912. Ivelich recalls that the old man took raw fillets of fish around to tables to sell customers on their freshness. He was so eager to please that if he lacked the fish he would undertake a special shopping expedition to the fish company across the street.

Present owners Steve and Bob Buich are the sons of Louis Buich, one of three brothers to immigrate from the Dalmatian coast and share ownership of Tadich's.

Sam's Grill (see page 72) was named for Sam Zenovich, who came from the Montenegro end of the Dalmatian coast. Its present owners are Walter and his father Gary Seput, son of Walter Seput, Sr., a Dalmatian who took over the restaurant in 1937.

Maye's Oyster House (1233 Polk Street) has been in Slav hands for more than seventy years, according to present owners Ned Boban, Dave Berosh, and Tony Simini. Boban was born in Dalmatia; Berosh is the son of a Dalmatian.

Chris Kriletich, a native of the island of Kortula on the Adriatic Coast, founded Chris's Seafood (694 Mission Street) in 1918. His widow, Onorina Kriletich, owned the restaurant until it was taken over by her daughter, Pat Kriletich.

Some general rules for cooking in the Dalmatian mode, according to the chefs at Tadich's and Chris's: "The simpler we make the fish, the better it comes out," and, "Always undercook. Never overcook. And serve immediately." Another chef adds, "Fish is fish. There are no recipes."

Some things chefs won't tell about their cooking. But some of the less secret ways are revealed in the following recipes.

Adapted from Gerald Adams, "A Special Way with Fish," *California Living Magazine,* February 1, 1976, pp. 25–31.

Sand Dabs and Rex Sole, Fried on a Grill

Clean and de-head fish. Dip in cracker meal or flour and place on a flat grill, medium hot (375 degrees), on a little vegetable oil, which can be seasoned with paprika, salt, and pepper, or lard.

Cook 3 to 5 minutes per side. Debone the fish by whacking off the tail with an extra stiff spatula, then running spatula along either side of backbone. If flesh seems too moist or translucent, place fillets in warm (not hot) oven for a minute or two. Figure three sand dabs or two sole per person.

Dominic Ivelich's Fried Sand Dabs

Ivelich, now retired from Tadich's likes to cook all fish in a ridge-bottomed cast-iron pan broiler. He pre-heats the pan for 5 minutes, rolls the sand dabs in flour seasoned with salt, pepper, and paprika, then fries the fish without oil over medium heat, 5 minutes per side.

Charcoal Broiled Fish

This method of cooking fish dishes is traditional on the Dalmatian coast.

At the San Francisco Dalmatian restaurants using this method, chefs use Mexican charcoal because they say it retains heat better than briquettes. They ignite the coals at least one hour before cooking time. No trace of flame remains. The coals are both a glowing red and gray in color.

For sea bass, use a steak 1 to 2 inches thick; dip in vegetable oil mixed with paprika, salt, and pepper. For a thicker slice, grill up to 10 minutes each side, 3 or 4 inches above the coals; a shorter time and closer to the coals if thinner. If you're afraid that fish will burn or dry out if kept too long on the coals, place fish in a 400-degree oven for the final 5 minutes, using a pan to which you have added a couple tablespoons of fresh lemon juice.

For salmon steaks: 5 minutes per side for a 1-inch thick steak. For rex sole (whole, in skin): about 3 minutes per side. For swordfish: 5 minutes per side. Times vary slightly according to the heat of the coals and proximity of grate.

Boiled Sea Bass Dalmatian

The classic method of cooking fish, other than the *gradele* or charcoal broiled method, is that of boiling. Actually the fish is simmered gently in a simple court bouillon.

Dominic Ivelich's Boiled Sea Bass Dalmatian

Water sufficient to cover fish in saucepan
1 clove garlic
2 bunches green onions, cut up
1 stalk celery, diced
Salt to taste
Potatoes (optional)
2 bass steaks, weighing ½ pound each

Simmer the water with all ingredients except fish for ½ hour; add fish. Cover, and cook until fish flakes at the touch of a fork — 10 or more minutes, figuring 10 minutes per inch of thickness. Serve with lemon.

Ned Boban's Boiled Sea Bass Dalmatian

Juice of ½ lemon
2 cups water
2 stalks celery, cut up
1 onion, cut in half
Dash of olive oil
Salt and pepper to taste
1 tomato, chopped (optional)
1 or 2 thick slices fresh sea bass

Combine all items but sea bass in a saucepan. Simmer 20 to 30 minutes. Add fish and simmer, covered, until done — 10 minutes or more. Figure 10 minutes per inch of thickness.

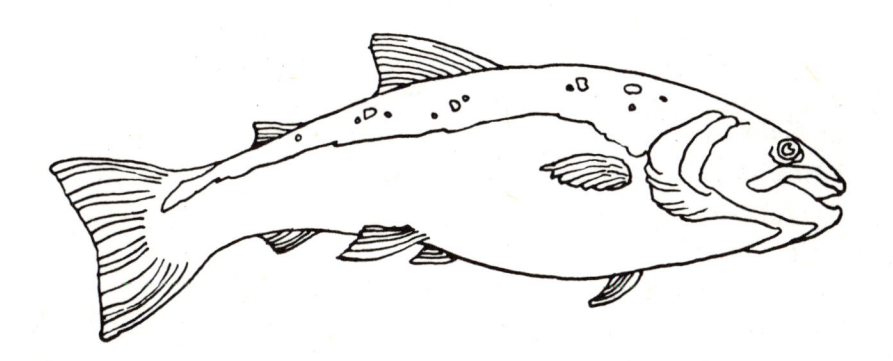

Ernie Aviani's Cioppino

1 onion, sliced
1 clove garlic, chopped
Olive oil, to brown onion and garlic
  2 tablespoons red wine vinegar
  1 live crab, disjointed
12 uncooked prawns
12 fresh clams
  1 can solid-pack tomatoes (large size)
Salt and pepper to taste
¼ teaspoon celery salt
Dash of paprika
Dry sherry to taste
  4 slices fresh sea bass
  1 cup chopped parsley

    Sauté onion and garlic in olive oil. When golden, add wine vinegar. Simmer one minute, then add crab, prawns, and clams. Sauté on low flame for 10 minutes, stirring occasionally. Add tomatoes, salt, pepper, celery salt, paprika, and sherry to your taste. Bring to simmer, add fish, cover, and cook 15 minutes, or until fish is done. Top with parsley. Serve with French bread.

    Although commonly regarded as a concoction of Italian fishermen at Fisherman's Wharf, this sort of dish, like bouillabaisse to the French or *zuppa di pesce* to the Italians, is no stranger to the Dalmatians, many of whom call it *brodetto*.

    Serves six to eight.

Basic Recipes

Hollandaise Sauce

5 egg yolks
2 small lemons
Dash of hot sauce
Dash of Worcestershire sauce
1½ cups warm clarified butter

Place a tureen into a pan of previously boiling hot water. Allow tureen to heat for 1 minute. Break egg yolks into tureen. Add strained juice of 1¼ lemons. Do not use bottled lemon juice. Add hot sauce and Worcestershire sauce. Beat or whip vigorously. While continuing to whip, slowly add warm clarified butter. Sauce will thicken. Add more lemon to taste, if desired.

Cream Sauce

2 tablespoons butter
2 tablespoons flour
1 cup cream
Salt and pepper to taste

Heat butter in saucepan. Blend in flour, and cook until bubbly. Add cream gradually, stirring constantly. Cook until thickened. Add salt and pepper. To thicken, use more butter and flour. To thin, use less butter and flour.
Makes 1 cup.

Brown Sauce

2 tablespoons butter
2 tablespoons flour
1 cup beef stock, or instant or cube bouillon and water
Salt and pepper to taste

Heat butter in saucepan. Blend in flour. Stir over low heat until flour is brown. Add beef stock gradually, and cook until thickened, stirring constantly. Add salt and pepper.
Makes 1 cup.

Fish Stock

1 tablespoon butter
1 tablespoon chopped onion
1 tablespoon chopped carrot
1 tablespoon chopped turnip
Fish bones, head, tail, and fins
1 stalk of celery
Sprig of parsley
Sprig of thyme
1 bay leaf
1 tomato, or a slice of lemon
1½ quarts water
Salt and pepper to taste

Put butter, onion, carrot, and turnip in a saucepan. Fry them without browning, then add fish bones, head, and trimmings, celery, parsley, thyme, bay leaf, and tomato or lemon slice. Cover with water, and let simmer for an hour or more. Season with salt and pepper. Strain.

Tartar Sauce

1 cup mayonnaise
1½ tablespoons sweet pickle relish
1 chopped green onion
1 teaspoon lemon juice

Combine all ingredients and chill. Keep refrigerated.

Cocktail Sauce

1¾ cups catsup
6 tablespoons water
1 teaspoon white wine
¼ teaspoon Worcestershire sauce
2 or 3 drops of hot sauce

Combine all ingredients and chill. Keep refrigerated.

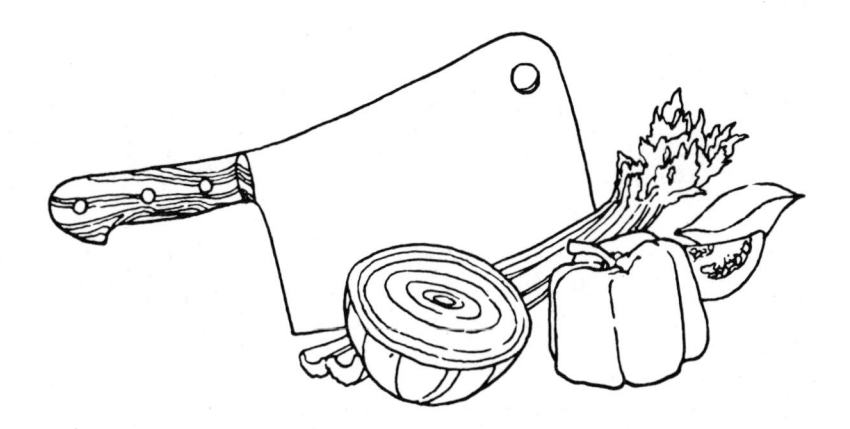

How To Buy a Fish

Fish products, high in protein, are a major source of food in this country. But while there is mandatory inspection of meat and poultry to insure that consumers buy safe and wholesome products, there is no required inspection of fish and fishery products. As a result, you must really be a more selective and informed shopper when selecting seafood. But how?

To help you determine quality when buying fish, the United States Department of Commerce's National Marine Fisheries Service (NMFS) has developed a list of things to look for in determining whether seafood is safe and fresh. This list is the same one used by federal inspectors under a new voluntary fish inspection program, which NMFS is conducting. Under the program, fish processors and canners can pay for federal inspectors to examine their fish and certify that they have been found to be safe, wholesome, and of a good quality.

Fishery products certified under the voluntary inspection program carry on their packages inspection marks indicating quality.

NMFS estimates that about 30 percent of the fishery products processed in the United States are inspected under the new program. These include canned tuna and these frozen items: fried fish, fish cakes, fish dinners, breaded shrimp, scallop products, and seafood platters. However, most fresh fish is not inspected because the consumer can see, touch, and smell it to determine its freshness. But to do this, you need to know what to look for.

Adapted from *Consumer News,* Vol. 5, No. 18, Sept. 15, 1975 (Washington, D.C.: Department of Health, Education, and Welfare).

Selecting Fresh Seafood

Fish

1. First look at the eyes, which should be bright, clear, and protruding slightly from the head. If the eyes have sunken into the head, the fish is probably not fresh.
2. Next check the gills. They should be bright red or pink. As quality slips, the gills begin to darken.
3. If the fish is gutted, turn it over and look at the intestinal cavity, which should be pink and have a fresh, clean appearance.
4. Any fresh cut of fish should have firm flesh, which will spring back when gently pressed with your finger. The skin should be shiny, and the fish should have a mild, clean odor.

In addition to determining the freshness of the fish, you must also decide what form of fish to buy. Fresh fish is usually sold in these forms:

- Whole or round fish. If you select this form, you must scale and gut the fish before you cook it. You will probably be able to use about 60 percent of the fish once it is scaled and gutted and once the head, tail, and fins are removed.
- Dressed. This form of fish is cleaned (scaled with the head, tail, and fins removed) and ready to cook. Since it still has the bones and skin, you will be able to eat about 80 percent of this form.
- Fish steaks. This form consists of cross-section slices of a large, dressed fish. Once you remove the bones, you can use about 90 percent of this form.
- Fillets. This form consists of slices of fish, cut away from the backbone and ready to cook. In this form, you can use 100 percent of the fish.

In deciding which form of fish to buy, NMFS suggests that you consider the cost per edible pound in terms of both convenience and waste. With fish that are bony or hard to prepare, it may pay to buy a form that, although more expensive per pound, has more edible flesh.

Crabs and Lobsters

If crabs or lobsters are fresh, look for movement of the legs. If there is no movement, they are probably dead. Don't buy.

Clams and Oysters

• Clams and oysters should be alive when bought in the shell. If the shells are closed, the shellfish are alive. If the shell is open, tap it gently to see if it closes. If it doesn't, the shellfish is probably dead and should be rejected.

• Check shucked oysters for plumpness and to see if they have a natural creamy color and are in a clear liquid.

Shrimp

Fresh shrimp is sold "green" — raw and in the shell, with or without head.

Frozen Seafood

Fish

- Make sure the fish is solidly frozen and has no objectional odor.
- Frozen fish may be glazed (dipped in water one or more times and quickly frozen to produce an icy glaze that protects the fish from dehydration). As long as the glaze remains intact and the fish remains frozen, it will keep well. If the glaze has melted or is chipped, the unprotected fish may turn a cottony white. This effect is called "freezer burn" and, even though the fish is still frozen, the exposed flesh has begun to suffer a cellular breakdown and should be rejected.
- Avoid damaged packages. Fish is packed in moisture and vaporproof materials to prevent dehydration and contamination. If the package is damaged, it could mean quality loss. Also, don't buy packages stacked above the freezing line in the store freezer. They may be thawed or in the process of thawing.

Shrimp

Frozen shrimp is sold according to color and count size — the smaller the size of the shrimp, the less expensive per pound. Count size per pound should be listed somewhere on the package. The sizes run: 1–5 shrimps, 6–10, 11–15, 16–20, 21–25, 26–30, 31–35, 35 shrimp or more.

Canned Seafood

• Check the condition of the can. If it is bulging, something has broken the seal, and the fish may be spoiled. If the can is dented or rusty, there is no way to know if the seal has been broken.
• When you open the can, check to make sure that the flesh is firm. If the meat is overcooked, the flesh next to the can will be darker. In this case, return the fish to the store.
• If the fish is packed in oil, the oil should be clean, not milky. Also, the can should be properly filled to the top. If it isn't, it should be returned.
• When buying canned tuna, be a label watcher. Albacore is the only kind of tuna that can be labeled "white meat." "Light meat" tuna comes from the yellow fin, skip jack, and blue fin varieties. If the can contains bonita, a fish very much like tuna, it must be labeled "bonita."

Storing Fish

Once you have made your fish selection and have brought the product home, how can you keep it? According to the NMFS you can follow several steps to help retain the quality of fishery products until you use them.
• Store canned products away from heat. When you open them, remove the contents from the can and store in glass or plastic container.
• To freeze fresh fish, divide the fish into small portions and then double wrap it to eliminate air. You can insure a good seal by folding the open end of the wrap several times. Then lay the fish flat in the freezer to freeze it quickly.

How to Prepare Live Crabs and Lobsters

Crabs and lobsters have usually been boiled when you purchase them from the dealer. However, if you buy live fish, drop them into a pot of boiling water and allow them to cook for 20 or 30 minutes, according to size. Add a tablespoon of salt for each gallon of water, and cover the pot.

Crabs and lobsters should be killed by immersion in boiling water. Do not accept uncooked shellfish unless they are alive.

Abalone

The abalone is found along the California coast. The coastal waters shelter green, black, and pink abalone, but it is the red abalone that is of commercial importance.

The abalone is 7 inches or more in its greatest diameter. It has a very strong shell. With the assistance of a large muscular foot, which forms almost the entire contents of its shell, it is able to exert a tremendous pressure by which it holds itself onto the rocks.

Abalone steaks should be well pounded in order to make them tender enough to be palatable. Since the law prohibits the shipping of this shellfish from the state, the people of California may enjoy abalone to the fullest extent.

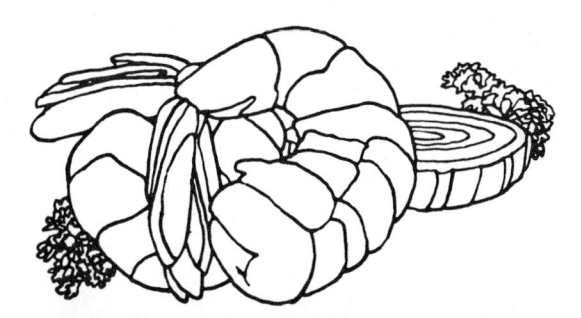

Best Bay Area Seafood Markets

Chinatown offers the best chance for fresh seafood, some of which can be brought home live, swimming in a bucket. (To procure live trout for *truite au bleu,* however, you must contact a fish hatchery, or catch them yourself at Lake Lagunitas in Marin.) Chinatown prices tend to be lower and its varieties most unusual, with live Dungeness and soft-shelled crab, fresh anchovies, abalone, terrapin, and tiny cockles. But you need to be finicky even in Chinese fish stalls.

At Fisherman's Wharf, you'll no longer see fish for the tourists, though it's easy to stop for a live crab or a Maine lobster (from **Fisherman's Seafood Inc., Pier 47, 776–6727**). Although the dockside warehouses behind Jefferson Street and at the foot of Leavenworth are nominally wholesale, you may find it profitable to scout these places in the mornings for "leftovers."

The city holds many excellent seafood sources, so don't give up when one highly respected purveyor tells you "there are no fresh bay scallops or sea urchins in San Francisco" or "fresh salmon is out of season."

Request special filleting jobs and order even ubiquitous sole in advance. Ask for the trimmings, frames, and heads to use for stock, chowder, and sauce bases. Present the fish eye, as the Chinese do, to a venerated elder. To protect freshness, carry a cooler when you're not going directly home from the fishmongers. Once home, refrigerate your purchase — on ice.

American Fish Market
1790 Sutter
921-5154

The American Fish Market carries an extensive inventory of produce and staples. Its long fish counter easily satisfies demands for hard-to-find fresh cod, sea urchin, and salmon roe, for salted mackerel, salmon, and pike. The horsetail clam, nature's X-rated shell, is more fascinating than a Mitchell Brothers' movie. *Sushi* is wrapped up at a bar in the corner of the store for take-out.

Antonelli's
Cal Mart Super Market
3585 California Street
752-7413

Antonelli's provides yet another good reason to visit this exceptionally fine supermarket patronized by Presidio Heights shoppers who demand high quality and good service and don't flinch at paying for it. Tony Antonelli, who owned a Market Street fish emporium before opening this shop, selects his local fresh fish daily (always lots of petrale sole, the best-seller) and imports Mexican prawns and Australian lobster tails.

California Sunshine Company
2171 Jackson
567-8901

Swedish-born Dafne and Mats Engstrom are building a caviar empire on the West Coast. Frustrated with the difficulties of finding enough good caviar at affordable prices, they have been working with marine biologist Serge Doroshov of the University of California at Davis to stock their own sturgeon ponds. "We have our first fish swimming up there now," says Dafne, "and I feel like a grandmother." These fish won't produce caviar for at least five years, even if the team is able to speed up the maturation process. Meanwhile, the Engstrom's are importing a bit of Oregon caviar, already earmarked for longtime customers such as New York's Four Seasons restaurant. The Engstroms are very excited about a new offering, a fresh whitefish roe, whose light orange color and lovely mild flavor have been hailed by food giants Craig Claiborne and James Beard. California Sunshine also sells crayfish and this summer will begin selling its own smoked salmon and smoked sturgeon.

Canton Market
1135 Stockton
982-8600

Curried crab and light, tender fish balls are among the deli specialties available almost daily in this market known, like the nearby Sang Sang, for having one of the most extensive arrays of gleamingly fresh fish (much of it moderately priced) in town. Unlike most fish markets, however, the Canton smells good, and the floor is not awash with brine.

D'Angelo Brothers
2339 Noriega
661-1438

This market has one of the best reputations in town. They try to keep prices reasonable on their fine selection of fresh fish, brought in daily: seabass, sturgeon, rock cod, salmon, trout, sand dabs, rex sole, to name but a few fins.

Dupont Market
1100 Grant Avenue
986-3723

Bustling with action, the Dupont is one of the most interesting and oldest stores on Grant Avenue, old enough to bear the street's original name. Customers tend to be loyal — as is the former San Franciscan who orders her roast duck shipped to her in Minnesota. The Dupont will vacuum-seal roast duck or chicken for anyone who wants to carry it or send it by air. You'll find every local fresh fish and five imported from the Philippines; abalone, scallops, salmon, clams, prawns, enormous crabs, fresh Petaluma ducks, quail eggs; tongues, brains, intestines, neckbones, tails, and spleen from the pig; Smithfield ham; Vietnamese sausages —*jolua* (pork) and *giolua* (beef); and rock-salt chicken that has been plunged into extremely hot rock salt to seal in the juices.

El Pescador Fish Market
3150 24th Street
647–2440

Open only since late 1979, this cheery shop has some offbeat selections such as small shark, catfish, Eastern oysters, bonita, bangus (popular in Filipino cooking), and king fish, as well as the more expected crabs, lobsters, prawns, and red snapper (rockfish).

Excelsior Fish and Poultry
4555 Mission Street
334–6106

Displaced Easterners will be thrilled at the catch in this well-known market, which carries not only the best Pacific Coast seafood but also imports a wide variety from around the country: Florida pompano, Maryland oysters, the basslike croaker, Louisiana buffalo fish and fresh-water catfish, white and large-mouth bass, Speigel carp, Idaho trout, Virginia scallops, and steelhead salmon from Oregon and Washington. It's hard to beat the assortment, including common local fish as well as mahi mahi (which tastes much like swordfish and can be prepared similarly), octopus, and squid. Excelsior's fish and poultry is sold at the outlets listed below, too, but you'll have a greater range of choices if you take the time to visit this Outer Mission District jewel.

Outlets

Grand Central Market, 2435 California, 931–4326, 346–7503
Lick Super, 350 7th Avenue, 386–4535
Petrini Plaza, Fulton and Masonic, 567–3855.
United Fish and Poultry.

Serramonte Fish and Poultry, 90 Serramonte Center, Daly City, 755–6046
Stonestown Fish and Poultry, 255 Winston Drive, 681–5380

La Rocca's Oyster Bar
3519 California
387–4100

You can buy fresh trout, sand dabs, rex sole, petrale, prawns, scallops, shad roe, or oysters to cook at home, or you can order them prepared in this rather tony setting. Toss in a salad and a glass of wine and call it lunch. You'll be in good hands: The owners were trained at Swan's.

Lee Sang Fish Market
1207 Stockton
989–4336

The market sometimes has fresh frogs and terrapin in addition to a big selection of fish — which will be cleaned if you request it.

Mainely Lobster
2183 Greenwich
567–3437

Open seven days a week, this small, attractive, gourmet market "specializes in live Maine lobster and fine Atlantic and Pacific seafood." Translation: clams, mussels, Australian lobster tails, frozen soft shell crabs, scrod, stuffed quahogs, and friendly service. They offer weekly specials and will also dress fish in fancy party clothes for special occasions.

Marine Delights
P.O. Box 12191
San Francisco 94112
239-7512

If you see a seven-foot lobster cruising Montgomery and California streets, go up and shake its claw. It's part of a promotion gimmick for Marine Delights, a discount seafood delivery outlet. With orders of five pounds or more of any fresh local high-quality seafood, Marine Delights will deliver free anywhere in the city. Biggest sellers are the lobster, petrale, and crab meat (not whole crabs), which they will gladly wrap in temperature-controlled coolers for shipping or carrying along. (Telephone orders only.)

Pioneer Market
3318 Mission
647-4300

The seafaring half of this no-nonsense family-owned butcher shop is possibly even more impressive than the landlubbers' side with 96 varieties of fresh fish available almost daily — would you believe fresh Louisiana catfish? They also sell prawns, scallops, and shrimp, but steer away from expensive shellfish.

Rossi's
Valley Pride Market
476 Castro Street
431-1128

Known for choice selections and a helpful attitude, Joe Fisher will take the trouble to debone chicken at no extra cost, for example, or roll and stuff petrale with shrimp. Also available: rabbit, fresh herbs, caul fat, and fresh veal sweetbreads. Fisher will also order anything for you, including big freezer offers.

S & S Fish Imports
2181 Irving
661-5050

Fresh tuna for *sashimi,* geoduck (horse clams), snow crab meat, live crab, Maine lobster, and fresh fish abound in this hole-in-the-wall, where you can also find a few Oriental dry goods (rice, ginseng).

Sang Sang Fish Market
2687 Mission
282-9339

1143 Stockton
443-0403

Part of the fun of shopping at these markets is watching dextrous employees reach into the saltwater bin of wriggling crabs and pull out a live one. At the Chinatown store, the daily specials are printed in Chinese on the wall, but don't worry: Some English is spoken at both stores. If the weather isn't too rough, Sang Sang will have fresh anchovies and is also excellent for fresh abalone, mussels, Blue Point crabs, brine shrimp, fish heads for chowder-making, squid, and Monterey prawns with roe still inside. If it swims in water, Sang Sang probably has it.

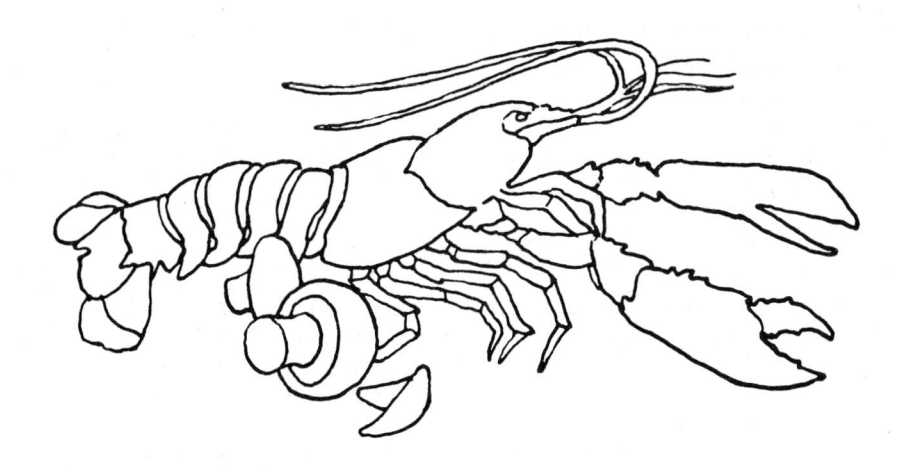

Sunset Super
2425 Irving
566–5362

Reputed to have the best fish in the Sunset District, Sunset Super doesn't sacrifice quantity for quality. In addition to a great deal of knowledge and patience, they offer fillet of petrale sole, rock cod, "red snapper," rex sole, perch, butterfish, sturgeon, English sole, fresh Idaho trout, whole ling cod, ling cod steaks, ling cod fillets, and English kippers, plus crabs, prawns, East Coast scallops, and Pacific Coast Spiny lobsters — sometimes fresh, sometimes frozen — from Baja California. They also will prepare seafood dishes for you to pick up for dinner (petrale fillets rolled and stuffed with shrimp, crab thermidor, and others) and share their recipes.

Swan Oyster Depot
1517 Polk Street
673–1101, 673–2757

Sal Sancimino and his sons have been dishing out jokes and excellent seafood from behind their long narrow bar forever. At Swan's, usually the only store in town for tiny fresh bay scallops and crayfish, the brothers six even make their own caviar for you to take home or eat at the counter with oyster crackers. The finest, liveliest — and costliest — fish depot in town, Swan's is not the place to shop if you have to ask the price. Noted for personal service, Swan's is always packed with loyal devotees who want care, attention, and advice with their fresh, already cracked crab.

Tokyo Fish Market
1908 Fillmore
931–4561

This miniscule family-run operation manages to squeeze produce baskets and a fish counter between its well-filled shelves. When they're not busy, the friendly owners will clean your squid and slice your *sashimi*.

Uoki Sakai
1656 Post Street
921–0515

On Saturdays, this bustling supermarket is busier than Tokyo, for it contains every ingredient necessary for the Japanese kitchen — and then some. What may be the world's largest box of Hershey's kisses is a prize on one of the shelves. Produce is fresh, and the broad sweet Japanese chives beg to be taken home and freely used. The fishmongers are as deft as *sushi* chefs. Hawaii is represented with *poi*, king's bread, and huge buckets of *takuan* (pickled radishes). Prolong your life as you navigate the crowded aisles by purchasing the package of spices to mix with sake for *toso*, the ninth-century Japanese New Year's drink thought to enhance longevity.

Ver Brugge Meats
3939 24th Street
647-8723

How can you resist a store so intent on freshness that they send their own boat out to catch salmon, thus providing such delicacies as salmon roe and salmon livers in season? Ver Brugge's is also known for quality beef (you won't believe the low prices on sirloin chops), smoked bacon, good lamb value, and a butcher who is obliging about special cuts such as *paupiettes*.

East Bay

Berkeley Fish, 1504 Shattuck Avenue, Berkeley, 845-7166

Great Atlantic Lobster Company, live Maine lobster. Clay Street Pier, Oakland, 834-2649.

Sprenger's Fish Grotto, 1919 4th Street, Berkeley, 845-7771

Sportsmen's Cannery, 67th & Hollis Avenue, Emeryville, 665-2282. Sells and smokes sportfishermen's salmon.

Marin County

Caruso's, Foot of Harbor Boulevard, Sausalito, 332–1015

Johnson Oyster Company, Point Reyes, 669–1149

Marin Poultry Company, 34 Greenfield Avenue, San Anselmo, 453–3622

Ocean Traders, 2000 Brideway, Sausalito, 332–2887

Rose's Oyster Depot, 21 Tamalpais Avenue, San Anselmo, 456–9825

Sabella's Oyster Bar and Fish Market, 9 Main Street, Tiburon, 435–2814

Tomales Bay Oyster Company, Point Reyes, 663–1242

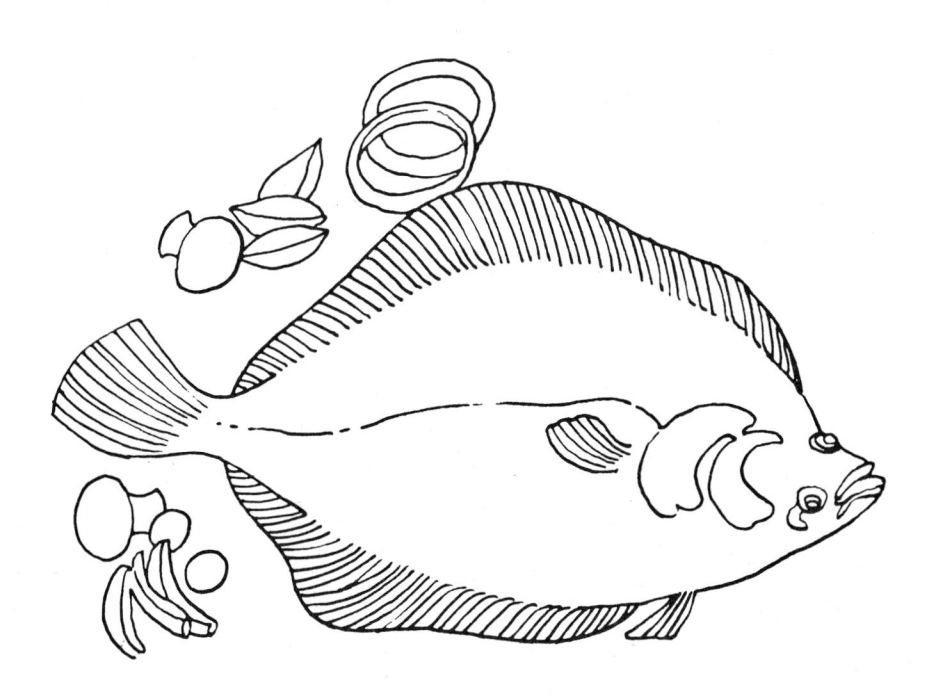

Index of Recipes

Abalone:
  Bordelaise, 78
  Steak, Fried, 87
Agnolotti, 46
  Dough, 47
Beef:
  Shabu-Shabu, 35
  Zwiebelfleisch (Grilled Tenderloin with Onions), 58
Bouillabaisse, 82
Broth, Basic Japanese, 35
Calamari:
  Calabresse, 16
  con Pomodoro (with Tomatoes), 11
  Salad, 37
  Sautéed, 17
  Sicilian Style, 17
Canneloni (with Seafood Filling), 76
Carp, Sweet and Sour, 44
Ceviche, 38
Chawan-Mushi (Egg Custard), 34
Chicken:
  Curry, 32
  Lemon, 104
  Pgules au Whiskey, 55
Chile con Queso, 56
Cioppino:
  Crab, 24
  Ernie Aviani's, 114
  Lazy Man's, 94
  Sauce, 27, 94
Clams:
  Chowder, 81

Elizabeth, 72
Vongole Bianco (with Spaghetti), 19
Cod. *See* Ling Cod; Rock Cod
Crab:
　Cioppino, 24, 94, 114
　Creole, 18
　Deviled Crab a la Sam, 73
　Fumet, 26
　Legs Sauté, 10, 30
　Mornay, 25
　Mornay en Casserole, 9
　Newburg Supreme, 68
　with Spaghetti, 66
　and Turbot, 93
Crayfish, 101
Desserts:
　Italian Cream, 39
　Neptune's Palace Delight, 53
Duck, Wild, 92
Fisherman's Stew, 79, 99. *See also* Bouillabaisse.
Fish Stock, 116
Frittata ala Louis, 88
Gyoza (Japanese Egg Roll), 49
Halibut with Egg Sauce, 21
Lamb, 106
Ling Cod, 38
Lobster:
　Sautéed Tails, 8, 20
　Thermidor, 15
Okra, Fried, with Cumin, 31
Oysters:
　alla Salvadori, 12
　Hangtown Fry, 74
Papillote, 102
Prawns:
　ala Szechwan, 83
　Bar Balued, 18

138/ Index

    Chinese Shrimp Scampi, 63
    Jumbo, Sauté Marsala, 29
    Patriced, 70
Rice Pilaff, 40
Rock Cod:
    California, 101
    Sweet and Sour, 41, 44
Salad:
    Calamari Salad, 37
    Dressing, Seafood, 28
    Frankie's Special, 10
Salmon:
    a l'Orlando, 71
    Broiled, 79
    Broiled Fillets with Hollandaise, 62
    Charcoal Broiled, 111
    Sweet and Sour, 86
Sand Dabs Fried 87, 111
Sauces:
    ala Creole, 14
    Bechamel, 26
    Bordelaise, 78
    Brown, 116
    Cioppino, 27, 94
    Cocktail, 117
    Cream, 115
    Egg, 22
    Fish Velouté, 103
    Ginger, 50
    Gyoza Dipping, 50
    Hollandaise, 115
    Hot Dip, 57
    Lamb, 107
    Light white, 47
    Meuniére, 89
    Mustard (Japanese), 51
    Napolitana, 77

Newburg, 15
Onion Purée, 59
Pesto, 90
Shabu-Shabu Dipping, 36
Soubise (Onion Sauce), 59
Sukiyaki, 97
Supreme, 67, 77
Sweet and Sour, 42, 45
Tartar, 117
Tempura, 98
Teppan Yaki, 50
Teriyaki, 95
Tomato, 91
Scallops:
  Broiled, 16
  Fu Yung, 42
  Morando, 62
  Sautéed, 52
  Sauté with Snow Peas, 54
Scampi, 48, 63
Sea Bass:
  Baked Visi Blanc, 20
  Baked with Shrimp, 23
  Boiled, Dalmatian, 112, 113
  Charcoal Broiled, 111
  with Egg Sauce, 21
Shabu-Shabu, 35
Shark, Thrasher, Sautéed and Capered, 100
Shrimp:
  Bisque, 7
  Paulette, 85
  Rarebit, 69
Snapper, 38
Sole:
  ala Via Reggio, 75
  Charcoal Broiled, 111
  Papillote, 102

Petrale Milanese, 13
Rex, Meunière with Capers, 89
Rex, and Sand Dabs, Fried, 111
Squid. *See* Calamari.
Sukiyaki, 96
　Sauce, 97
Sweet and Sour Fish, 44
Swordfish:
　Charcoal Broiled, 111
　Stuffed Antone, 66
Tempura:
　Batter, 98
　Sauce, 98
Teriyaki, 95
　Sauce, 95
Tripe, 90
Turbot:
　Crab and, 93
　Stuffed with Deviled Crab, 64
Veal:
　Paprika Schnitzel (Cutlets with Paprika), 61
　Rahm Schnitzel (Cutlets with Cream and Mushrooms), 60

NOTES

NOTES